ON MY WAY!

A Volunteer Firefighter/EMT's Story

BY

Lieutenant Dan McCann

Book design: Russel Davis
Photos: Dan McCann

ISBN: 979-8-218-36108-2

Printed in the Unites States of America

Risk a lot to save a lot,
risk a little to save a little,
and risk nothing to save nothing.

Chief Alan "Bruno" Brunacini
(1937-2017)

Contents

Preface

This book is a collection of short stories about some of the emergency calls I've been on as a volunteer firefighter in Spokane, Washington. My goal in writing the book was that my stories contain meaningful insights into what it's like to be a volunteer and, more specifically, what it's been like for me.

Throughout the book, I've done my best to describe the characters and events of each story accurately. I apologize if I've gotten anything wrong. While writing my stories, I've relied primarily on my memories and the memories of fellow volunteers at Station 96. In several instances, I also gathered information from public Internet sources, public information obtained from the Washington State Department of Natural Resources, and a small stack of unofficial handwritten records from Station 96.

I have used the real names of firefighters in each chapter because they are a matter of public record. However, all patients and victims described in the book are either nameless or were given fictitious names to protect their privacy.

As I wrote the early drafts of each story, I asked my wife and several Station 96 volunteers to read them. Their feedback was immensely helpful, supplementing and sometimes correcting my memories. Their comments helped me recall additional memories about each call. They also asked me to include more about my thoughts and feelings during and after each call, which I have tried to do.

The order of the stories in the book was sometimes merely a consequence of the order in which I wrote them. However, I have moved a few around to provide a bit of variety for the reader. Consequently, sequential chapters often present different types of calls that took place many years apart.

Although the book represents only two dozen or so calls occurring over 26 years of volunteering, I believe this small window into my efforts as a volunteer captures the essence of my career and, perhaps, motivates someone else to start theirs.

ON MY WAY!

Chapter 1

Never Again

In my early years of volunteering, I lived on Black Bear Lane, which is up on Forker Ridge. My home was about five miles from Station 96, and it took me seven to eight minutes in good weather to safely respond to the station. The first three miles of the drive were on gravel roads covered in washboard in the summer and snow and ice in the winter. In the first two miles, the road dropped from 3,200 to about 2,500 feet of elevation, making it likely my worn-out Ford Bronco II 4X4 would be skipping and sliding along on the gravel, threatening to put me into the ditch or off the outside edge of the road down into the trees below. The tight blind corners that populated the top of the ridge were, on their own, challenging to navigate. They were especially difficult if I was to also avoid crashing into unseen oncoming traffic. On a warm mid-summer day in 2001, I was at home on Black Bear Lane when I received a call for a 31D medical emergency that was happening about half a mile south of Station 96. Thirty seconds later, I was heading to the station in my Bronco.

As I pulled out of my driveway onto Black Bear Lane, I coached myself to relax, focus on my driving, and keep the wheels on the road. I drove as fast as I dared, bouncing and sliding over the graveled bumps and washboard. As I drove, I found myself wondering in frustration why I had not read the entire page so I would know the details of the call. Suddenly, I realized that by thinking about not reading the page, I was ignoring my coaching to focus on driving. I put it all out of my mind and drove carefully but purposefully.

The address of the call was on East Piper Road, which intersects with Forker Road about a half mile south of the station. As I approached the station from the south, I thought that if I bypassed Piper Road and drove on to the station, the odds were 100 percent Brush 96 (B96) would be gone when I got there. I decided to drive straight to the address of the incident hoping other volunteers would bring B96 with all of our medical gear. When I arrived on Piper Road, I was relieved to see B96 parked on one of the driveways on

Piper. I could see Captain Mike, Don, and a third person walking towards the front door of a small red clapboard house. I parked, jumped out of my car, and followed them in, donning my EMS gloves and safety glasses as I walked.

Once inside the house, Mike, Don, and I were led through a small, crowded bedroom to a tiny bathroom. The patient's name was Ed, an elderly man who had been using the toilet when he collapsed onto the bathroom floor. He was conscious but unable to move or speak. Ed's adult son, John, had come to visit him that morning and found him. He immediately called 911. John was the man that met us outside when we pulled up.

Ed built the house in 1929 and raised a family there. But now that his children are grown and his wife has passed, he lives alone. There was no way to know how long he had been on the floor.

Ed was lying on his right side, still in a sitting position, with his hips and knees bent at almost 90 degrees. His pants and underwear were down around his ankles. The bathroom was very small. So small, we had to slide Ed back towards the toilet to open the bathroom door. After both Mike and Don squeezed into the tiny room, I laid open our EMS bag on the bed. I assumed it would be my job to rifle through the bag and hand them whatever they needed. Mike was trying to communicate with Ed, while Don was beginning to try getting a set of vitals. Don suddenly turned and asked me to grab our suction device to see if I could get far enough into the bathroom to suction out the blood and sputum that had accumulated in Ed's mouth. I took to the task, but while trying to suction the small mass of dried blood and saliva, I suddenly noticed Ed staring at me. His face was emotionless, but his eyes were filled with anxiety. I paused, leaned closer to his ear, and told him in the calmest voice I could muster what I was about to do. I also told him the ambulance was coming and we would do everything we could to help him. As I spoke to him, I saw no sign of recognition or comfort in Ed's eyes. He continued to stare at me. My heart sank. I quickly dropped the suction device and used my gloved finger to sweep the blood and saliva out of his mouth. Just then, both the three-person crew from Engine 94 (E94) and the two-person crew from the ambulance squeezed into the bedroom.

The medic from E94 asked us to move Ed out of the bathroom onto the backboard they had placed on the bedroom floor. The plan was to strap Ed to the backboard, lift him, and carry him outside to the ambulance's gurney. This was going to be a quick "load and go."

We were all thinking of the so-called "golden hour" for stroke patients. It represents the first 60 to 80 minutes after a stroke when a patient responds best to intravenous thrombolytic therapy. The goal of the therapy is to limit the degree of brain damage by dissolving blood clots in the brain. Because we didn't know when the stroke occurred, there was a great sense of urgency to get Ed to the hospital quickly. I remember thinking how unlikely it was that it had been less than an hour since his stroke. I also hoped I was wrong.

As they secured Ed to the backboard, I noticed his right arm was extended along his side, and he nervously tapped his hand repeatedly against his thigh. In the wake of everything happening around him, Ed was helpless, but his hand was working overtime. He still looked anxious, but now he was staring at the ceiling. I remember wondering what he was thinking and asking myself: what would I be thinking if I were him?

Time seemed to stand still while I watched him tap, tap, tap, tap on his thigh. I felt the sudden urge to reach out and hold his hand to comfort him. But I didn't do it. I just watched. Tap, tap, tap, tap, over and over. Decades later, I can still picture him lying there, tapping his thigh, lying silently with a frightened look in his eyes. Remembering those last few minutes with Ed still puts a lump in my throat.

The next day, Ed died. He never regained the ability to speak or move.

I had only met Ed that one time, the day he had his stroke. Yet, when I heard he had died, I felt sad and defeated. I vowed to myself I'd never again be reluctant to physically reach out and give whatever comfort I could to one of our patients. I felt I had let Ed down and didn't want ever to do something like that again.

Several years after Ed's death, I met and married my wife, Karie. We lived in the log home I had built up on Forker Ridge for a couple of years, but in 2006, we bought a 20-acre parcel of heavy timber just east of Peone Prairie. The property was only 1 1/4 miles west of Station 96, so my responses to the station could be much easier and quicker. Together, we built our current home amidst the tall timber, and now it takes me only three minutes to get through the woods to the station: a far cry from the white-knuckled drive down Forker Ridge. We bought the land where we built our new home from a local man named John. John had recently inherited the property from his dad, Ed, who had lived on Piper Road in a small red clapboard house he'd built in 1929.

Chapter 2

Trying to Help People on the Worst Day of Their Lives

I once had a nursing student tell me something her nursing mentor told her, "Always remember, when you become a nurse, you will often be helping people on the worst day of their life. Remember that, and you'll always be a good nurse." The nursing student was enrolled in a sophomore-year course I was teaching at a local university in the Pacific Northwest. She told me this while butchering a cow's heart dissection in my anatomy lab. It was years ago, but my eyes well up even now when I think of that simple statement.

December 1, 2015, was the worst day of several people's lives. It was late on a cold, gray day when my pager went off for a 31D. The address was two miles south of Station 96. I quickly typed "On my way!" on my iPhone using our Station 96 text chain, threw on my Spokane County Fire District 9 jacket, and headed for the garage. When I reached the garage, incoming texts indicated Jon was heading straight to the scene, and Gary was responding to the station.

The outdoor temperature was below freezing, and I knew my logging road shortcut to the station was frozen but snowless, so I walked past my car, donned my helmet and gloves, and jumped on my Kawasaki KLX250. I can ride the bike to the station in less than four minutes, but frozen gravel and dirt can be treacherous, so it's a bit riskier this time of year. Even with the new knobby tires, I coached myself to hold back a little and not trust that the front tire would stick as I entered the corners. The ride was quick, bumpy, and bitter cold. My gloved hands and thighs were stinging from the cold when I finally reached the station. I climbed in Brush 96 and pulled out on the ramp to wait for Gary.

Sitting on the ramp, I looked at my pager, memorized the address, and noticed that the call had been upgraded to an "echo" call. The echo code told me CPR was in progress, and the District's EMS supervisor had been added to the call. Gary (our station Training Lieutenant) arrived a minute or two later, and we headed off with lights and sirens. Gary radioed dispatch and told them Brush 96 was responding. Dispatch replied that Engine 92 (E92) was already on scene. The patient was a 16-year-old female. CPR was in progress.

CPR on a 16-year-old is unusual and a bit disturbing. "Holy Shit," Gary said. Because of the echo upgrade, we anticipated we'd be assigned to establish a landing zone (LZ), be ground contact, and "land the bird": our local Med Star helicopter. We'd done this many times before and were confident it would go smoothly. Landing the bird never entered our minds again.

When we pulled up to the house, we were surprised to see multiple Sheriff's units were on scene. "What's up with SO being here?" I asked. "No idea," Gary replied.

Gary and I piled out of the truck while donning our EMS gloves and safety glasses. A Deputy Sheriff stationed outside the garage pointed to the door to his left. We nodded and entered the garage. The first thing I saw was another Sheriff standing over a large caliber revolver lying on the floor. My gaze immediately shifted to the medic and firefighter performing CPR in the middle of the concrete floor. Jon was the firefighter doing CPR. He had driven straight to the scene and arrived a minute before us. Gary and I have performed CPR numerous times, so we immediately cycled into the rotation of doing compressions, putting on electrocardiogram (ECG) leads, helping to establish an intravenous drip (IV), and doing whatever the medic asked us to do. I knelt next to Jon and replaced him. Gary and Jon melded into other supporting jobs.

Once I began performing compressions, I saw the patient for the first time. She was a blond teenager with a self-inflicted gunshot wound to her abdomen. The entry wound was a small round blood-filled hole halfway between her rib cage and umbilicus. The wound was not bleeding, which surprised me. Seeing it, I couldn't help imagining the shattered liver beneath that little puddle of blood. I shifted my gaze to the display on the Life Pack 1500 to distract myself and monitor the consistency of the rate and depth of my compressions.

A dark pool of blood soon began seeping from the exit wound on her back. I slowly shifted my knees away from the encroaching pool, not missing a beat. But very soon, my lower back began to ache from the awkwardness of my position. I knew I'd be replaced at the next two-minute mark, so I tried to ignore the pain. The next thing I remember thinking was that my CPR was not going to save this patient. Gary soon slid in next to me and took over. I slowly stood, wincing from the stiffness in my lower back. I was immediately handed the IV bag and told to gently squeeze it to ensure a maximal flow of saline disappeared into the patient's vein.

As the rounds of CPR continued, several other first responders joined us in the garage. The first was Jeff, our Fire District 9 EMS Supervisor. He became the official team leader. A two-person crew from the ambulance entered a minute later. The atmosphere in the garage shifted from urgency to somber work as the team leader calmly read out the time cues and commands that coordinate everyone.

The medic-in-charge soon called for intubation. The ambulance medic laid himself flat on the concrete floor and placed an endotracheal tube (ET) in the victim's throat and trachea. Once the ET tube was placed, Jon took over ventilating the patient with a bag-valve device. Everything was progressing smoothly, everything except the condition of the patient.

A moment later, the patient's parents, who had just arrived in their car, walked into the garage unannounced. Mom started screaming. A Sheriff quickly ushered them out. We kept our heads down and continued working.

A moment later, the patient's parents, who had just arrived in their car, walked into the garage unannounced. Mom started screaming. A Sheriff quickly ushered them out. We kept our heads down and continued working.

Ending a CPR protocol is never an easy thing to do. Especially when the patient is young with so much of their life ahead of them. Jeff, our team leader, discussed the situation with the other medics and then called medical control to consult with the doctor on duty. After discussing all the pertinent information with the doctor, Jeff went into the house and spoke with the parents. When he returned, he told us to terminate the protocol.

Gary, Jon, and I were emotionally exhausted after the call. Jon and Gary have daughters, which made it much closer to home for them. Over the next few days, we called and texted each other to help us process our feelings. We all know there is value in what we do as volunteers. But it isn't always obvious what that value is after a call like this one. Even now, years later, our minds can take us back to that garage. It's never easy; being on such a call never feels good. It just is what it is: difficult.

Years after this call, I still feel unsatisfied with what we did that day. Calls like that stay in your mind for years, and the unanswered questions remain: Who was she? Why did she do it? Could we have done anything more? How many more of these calls will I have to deal with?

Chapter 3

I Don't Think We're Gonna Catch It!

When a wildland fire burns, there are two characteristics: the intensity and rate of spread that determine how fast the fire grows. These two characteristics depend on four factors: (1) the wind velocity (a vector with properties of speed and direction), (2) the topography (the degree and aspect of the slope), (3) the fuel (the amount and type of fuel), and (4) the preheating of the fuels (affected by temperature, humidity, and time of day). When the wind, topography, fuel, and fuel preheating all enhance fire intensity and rate of spread, these factors are said to be "in alignment." On August 5, 2015, the conditions on the southwest slopes of the Foothills were very much in alignment. It was warm, dry, and windy. The high was 85 degrees, and the wind blew out of the southwest at 10 to 15 mph, with gusts reaching 30-plus mph all afternoon. Relative humidity (RH) had dropped below 15%. The southwest-facing slopes of the Foothills were baked dry and ready to burn.

It was 6:54 PM when a 14H vegetation fire (the 14 code indicates a vegetation fire, and the H signifies a high response) was dispatched for 9704 North Forker Road. I quickly texted, "On my way!" to our volunteer group text and headed for our shop. In the summer, my Kawasaki KLX250 is always parked in the shop, resting on its kickstand facing outwards for a quick getaway. As I grabbed the handlebars, I noticed my hands were shaking from anticipation. Standing beside the bike, I pulled in the clutch and hit the start button. The single-cylinder four-stroke engine fired up instantly. I checked that the bike was in neutral, released the clutch, and let the engine idle while I donned my helmet, goggles, and gloves. With a push on the handlebars, I stepped on the left foot peg, threw my right leg over the bike, clicked the transmission into first gear, released the clutch, and twisted the throttle. I was on my way down the driveway to the steep, curvy two-track trail that takes me to the station. About 30 seconds into my ride, I reached the shallow creek that runs through our property, crossing it with a refreshing cold splash of water. Instantly, I was hard on the throttle, climbing the steep bank that heads out to the county right-of-way. The seldom-used gravel and dirt right-of-way runs east through heavily timbered forest. Massive Doug Fir trees and thick hedges of brush outline the road. I navigated the many jumps and dips by standing on the pegs, soaking up the bumps with my legs while squeezing both knees against the gas tank for balance and stability. My KLX250 has nine inches of suspension travel, so it navigates the bumpy road well. But making good time still demands all of my skills and focus. I've no time to think about the fire.

The right-of-way is only wide enough for a single full-sized pickup, so if I meet one of my neighbors driving in the other direction, I would have to quickly find a spot off the road to wait for them to pass. Running head-on into a pickup truck while traveling 30 to 40 mph would be deadly, so I can't relax for a second. Luckily, the road was deserted.

I crested the last hill and left the forest behind, free to fly up the gravel road to the station. Arriving at the station, I saw Captain Don's truck parked in his usual spot. I realized we'd be the first unit on the scene and felt a tightening in my stomach.

Don lives east of Forker Road, and he told me later that while driving to the station, he had looked southwest toward the address on his pager to try and see the smoke column. But the horizon was clear. At the station, he quickly discovered the Forker Road address was the calling party's address. The fire was located at the east end of Macmahan Road, which meant he had been looking in the wrong direction. When he looked east of the station, the smoke column was impossible to miss.

Don and I donned our wildland gear and jumped into B96. I hit the remote control to open the bay door and pulled onto the ramp. The wind was blowing hard from the southwest, laying the smoke column over to the northeast and driving the fire up the steep draw. Seeing the dark building column, I knew our skills and fitness would be tested.

Because the call was a 14H, we knew we had other career-staffed brush trucks and engines from other District 9 stations responding. We also knew more volunteers would respond in Water Tender 96 (WT96) and E96. When Don radioed dispatch that we were responding, Dispatch replied with their short description of the incident, telling us the fire was a small outbuilding. Don turned to me and said, "That's *not* just a small outbuilding burning." Just then, Lieutenant Cody Traber, responding in Brush 94 (B94) from Station

94, radioed Dispatch. He reported it appeared from his location on Bigelow Gulch Road that the fire had not yet spread to the wildland. We were much closer to the fire than Cody and chuckled at his optimism.

We arrived on the scene at 7:05 PM, eleven minutes after the fire was dispatched. Macmahan Road ends in a small cul-de-sac bordered by a large two-story residence and a single-story manufactured home. A 40x80 metal building sits about 50 yards upslope and north of the manufactured home. The land surrounding the cul-de-sac rose steeply on the north, east, and south slopes at a 30% grade. The south and east slopes consisted of heavy Ponderosa Pine with a brush understory. The north slope was covered in light, fast fuels, primarily tall grass and young Ponderosa Pine.

Don radioed dispatch with his windshield size-up, "Dispatch, Brush 96 is on scene. We have a fully involved 12x12 structure. The fire has spread to the grass and brush. It's about one acre and moving up the draw behind the home. Brush 96 will be Macmahan Command and doing a progressive hoselay on the fire's west flank."

As dispatch confirmed Don's size up, Don pointed to a short driveway just north of the house. "Back us in right there," he said.

I drove up the short driveway, swung around, and backed into the spot. Don jumped out and started the pump while I donned my fire shelter, water bottles, and radio. I threw a 30-pound progressive hose pack on my back. I was wearing 45 pounds of gear as I glanced up at the fire. It was advancing up a 30% slope loaded with dry grass and brush. My heart was already racing as I anticipated the job ahead of us.

Don knocked down areas of fire next to the truck using one of the hose reels. He then knocked down enough fire on the hillside for us to start up the slope. I stepped to the 200-foot slot load of progressive hose, placed the first 100 feet on my right shoulder, grabbed the drag loop on the bottom 100 feet with my left hand, and pulled hard as I started to climb. I was now carrying 60 pounds of gear. Once I got up the embankment and away from the truck, I dropped the 100 feet of hose off my shoulder, laying it out in a pattern so it wouldn't turn into a tangled mess when we charged it. I signaled Don to charge the line, waited for the water to reach my nozzle, and then extinguished the fast-approaching flames in the grass and brush 20 feet away. By then, Don had donned his gear and progressive hose pack and started to help me drag the charged hose as we climbed the slope parallel to the fire front. We could see the head of the fire climbing ahead of us. For a minute, we both thought we might be able to catch the head of the fire. We were wrong.

After about three minutes of climbing, we were 200 feet up the slope and needed to add our first 100-foot section of hose from my progressive backpack. Don pulled the outer 100-foot roll from my pack and rolled it downhill away from the fire. I clamped the charged line shut using a large aluminum clamp and switched my nozzle to the newly laid hose. Don removed the hose clamp, returned it to my pack, and we moved up the slope, putting out the fire as we climbed. Even though we could see the head of the fire working its way up the slope, we were losing it. All we could do was keep climbing and spraying.

While we were working our way up the left flank, B94 radioed they were on the scene. Lieutenant Cody Traber was the officer on B94. He assigned his two firefighters to a progressive attack on the right flank, then jogged over to us and asked Don if he wanted to pass Command to B94. Don was glad to let Cody take over Command. Just before Don and I started back up the slope, I turned to Don and Cody and yelled over the roar of torching trees and brush, "I don't think we're gonna catch it!". They simultaneously shook their heads in agreement. Cody turned and hustled down the slope.

Don and I continued to put all our efforts into spraying water and climbing. We still had three hundred feet of hose in our packs, but the head of the fire had gotten far enough ahead we couldn't see it. Fortunately, we had progressed high enough on the slope to cut off any chance for the fire to run west and ignite the 40x80 shop on our left.

At 7:09 PM, Cody reported to dispatch the 12x12 structure was lost, and B96 and B94 were starting to get a knockdown on the one-acre fire. Just after Cody met with Don and me on the left flank, he reported to Dispatch that the fire had started to run up the draw. At 7:12 PM, he requested air support. His experience told him the fire would continue to grow, and he knew we wouldn't have a chance to stop it without air support.

What Cody didn't know when he asked for air support was that District 9's Fire Chief, Jack Cates, had already been on the radio (on a separate channel) with the Department of Natural Resources (DNR) for Eastern Washington asking for air support. Because of the fast action of Chief Cates, air support was assigned at 7:09 PM, three minutes before Cody asked for it.

A radio communication at 7:13 PM from Arcadia 61, a DNR overhead, went as follows:

7:13 PM, AR61: "I have just arrived on the fire and have a quick size up for you, one to two acres, west aspect, 30% slope in grass and brush and Ponderosa Pine, 3-5-foot flame lengths, fire is running and torching. Let's continue all incoming resources. Winds are 15-20 sustained with gusts to 25."

The fire was gaining momentum. It was only 18 minutes since the original dispatch, and everyone on the fire knew we wouldn't catch it anytime soon. More resources were badly needed.

At 7:08 PM, three minutes after Don and I arrived on the scene, Lieutenant Whitey Wentz from Station 96 arrived in WT96. Whitey, one of our seasoned volunteers with 20-plus years of experience, parked WT96 between B96 and B94. He quickly installed a pair of 2 ½-inch hoselines to fill both brush trucks simultaneously. Without his quick response, B96 and B94 would have been out of water in minutes.

Just after Whitey responded, Jon and Gary responded in E96. Gary is our Training Lieutenant, and Jon has about ten years of experience as a contract wildland firefighter. They arrived on the scene at 7:21 PM. Gary was assigned to work on the left flank with Don and me. Jon was assigned to man the pumps on B96 and B94. He also helped Whitey keep the brush trucks full of water. Only 27 minutes after the fire was dispatched, Station 96 had five volunteers and three trucks fighting the fire.

When Gary and Jon climbed the left flank, Don and I were working with Chief Jim Walkowski. Jim had come up the line to help extend our progressive hose line farther up the slope. We were 600 feet upslope and had used all the hose we had. Fortunately, a DNR crew had just hustled up the slope, bringing us four hundred feet of additional hoseline. Gary checked in with Don and then returned to B96 to grab two rolls of 1-inch hose. His assignment was to tie into the main hoseline and put out fingers of fire that increasingly threatened to burn over our hoseline. Jon also helped with Gary's assignment, splitting his time between this task and overseeing pump operations on the two brush trucks.

Jon was eventually sent to help with the progressive hoseline on the right flank. The two-man crew on B94 was struggling to deploy their hoseline through the thick "reprod" (thick clusters of young pine trees), forest litter (downed trees and branches from heavy winter snow), and thick mature Ponderosa Pine. The right flank hoseline needed to be zigged and zagged 600 feet up the steep draw around and through all these obstacles. Fortunately, the winds pushed the fire northeast away from the timber on the right flank.

Not long after Gary arrived, the fire on the left flank spotted over our wet line and started to wrap around below those of us working high on the left flank. I remember looking down the fire line to see fire climbing towards us in tall grass. My first thought was that this is how crews get burned over. I yelled a warning to Don and the rest of our crew. We retreated from the fire line and attacked the spreading fire below us. Fortunately, we got a quick knockdown before it wrapped around us.

To provide a broader perspective of the fire, below are selected radio communications between several DNR Incident Commanders and DNR's dispatch center. The reference to T852 refers to the first on-scene air resource, a WWII-era PBY airframe, a model Y Patrol Bomber converted to fight wildland fires. These selected communications demonstrate the challenges we faced over the next few hours.

7:43 PM: DNR Incident Command, "T852 is making drops on the left flank. We are trying to get a progressive hose lay on both flanks. Fire is still running up the canyon, spotting out ahead of itself, with group and individual torching."

7:45 PM: DNR Incident Command, "What do we have for additional aircraft? T852 is not able to keep up."

8:39 PM: DNR Incident Command, "We will stick with [an estimated size of] 7-10 acres. We've got crews building lines up both the left and right flanks and have extended the hand line to a progressive hose lay on the left flank. We did lose that flank, and the crews had to back off due to increased activity on the left flank. We are getting the dozer in there now. Winds are shifting on the ridge top. We've got crews on the right flank going direct with a hand line, and we've got the other dozer to reinforce that line on the right flank."

9:48 PM: "Right now, we will call the fire size 10 acres."

10:27 PM: "Left flank firing ops are going well. For the right flank, we are still taking hand line up counterclockwise around the fire. Currently, resources on the head of the fire are scouting for line locations. Fire is 15 plus acres."

11:34 PM: "At this time, estimating 20 acres…. The head is still active with torching."

1:32 AM: "We are holding at approximately 40 acres. The left flank of the fire is lined and burned out. The right flank is burned out. Currently working on putting in hand line around the head of the fire on the north aspect's heavy fuels and steep terrain. Crews working from both directions to trail with a hand line. We have dozers working north of their location working on establishing contingency line."

These communications show that the fire continued to grow despite all our efforts. A review of the weather records for the evening revealed that the temperature had dropped to 70 degrees by 10:00 PM, the winds were 12-14 mph, and the RH had increased moderately to 29%. Three hours into the evening, conditions had slowly improved but still had yet to cause the fire intensity to lessen as much as we had hoped.

Throughout the evening, Station 96 firefighters made numerous trips up and down the fire's flanks carrying hoses, fittings, and digging hand lines. We also spent time cooling off hot spots in the fire's interior. Eventually, we extended over 1,000 feet of hoseline to the top of the ridge, where the fire had slowed and was ultimately stopped by hand crews and air support. It had been a heck of a fight.

Thinking back on the fire, I remember that at one point, about an hour after we arrived on the scene, I had scampered down the left flank to retrieve another progressive hose pack. Because of the steepness of the slope, my thighs were burning from fatigue. I remember being disappointed in myself for being old and out of shape. My thighs and back were stiff and sore for three days after the fire.

Eventually, the fire was measured using a portable global positioning system (GPS) unit at 45 acres. During the following three to five days, several of us took shifts to shuttle water in WT96 to DNR and local fire crews that mopped up and fully contained the fire. I remember a moment the following day when I was using WT96 to fill a "pumpkin" (an orange portable inflatable water tank) for a DNR crew. We were on a dirt switchback on the north side of the ridge where the fire had been stopped. The view to the west was unobstructed, and I could see two large columns from other fires about 20 miles away. Large air tankers were working each fire and would occasionally fly low over the top of us going to and from Coeur d'Alene airport, where they reloaded with red fire retardant. Seeing it was impressive. I suddenly felt proud to be a part of the fire service.

At 45 acres, the Macmahan fire was not a large fire by state standards. But the fire certainly had the potential to grow to hundreds, if not thousands, of acres. There were four factors that stopped it from becoming a much larger fire. The first was the fire started in the early evening, and conditions for fire growth decreased in the next three to five hours. The second was the fire was caught at the ridge top when it transitioned from an upslope running fire to a downhill backing fire. The third was that the fire was not in a remote wilderness area, so the first units arrived in minutes. The final factor was the commitment and skill of a small group of volunteer and career firefighters who live and work in the foothills of Mt. Spokane. This is their community, and they are committed to doing everything they can to protect it. So, regardless of where you live, give a wave of thanks the next time you see a local fire apparatus pass by. They deserve it.

Chapter 4

It's the Nightmare House!

It was Sunday, April 19, 2012, at about 5:30 PM. My wife, Karie, and I were returning home from dinner. We were five miles west of our property when we noticed a thick black column of smoke rising from the base of the Foothills due east of us. I was wearing my fire department pager, but it hadn't gone off, which was odd. So, I pulled out my phone and called Mike Atwood, a Fire District 9 Fire Commissioner, who lived about halfway between where we were and the smoke column. Mike had been a volunteer at Station 96 for decades before retiring and becoming a Fire Commissioner for Spokane County Fire District 9 (SCFD9). When he answered my call, he was unaware of the smoke. While we spoke on the phone, he walked out onto his deck.

"Wow, that's quite a column. What do you think it is?"

The words had just left his mouth when my pager and his pager went off simultaneously. It was an 11F, a code indicating a structure fire.

"I gotta go, Mike," I said.

"Yeah, I guess you do," he replied.

I ended the call and drove straight towards the station, trying not to speed.

When Karie and I arrived at the station, E96 sat on the ramp, ready to go. Don and Whitey were in the front seats, Whitey was driving. Gabe, a new volunteer, was in the back seat.

I pulled into the station parking lot and stopped in a cloud of dust. I kissed Karie goodbye. "Have fun and be safe," she said. I jumped out and trotted by the engine into the bay. "We'll wait for you," Don yelled as I passed. He had seen two more volunteers, Jon and Gary, pulling up right after me and knew they would take WT96.

As I climbed into my boots and donned my turnouts, Jon came in and started getting ready. Gary then burst through the door. He had driven by the fire on his way to the station.

"It's the nightmare house. We'll bring the tender. You're gonna need water!" he said loudly.

"Sounds good," I said as I walked out to the bay.

As I headed for the engine, I asked myself, "What the fuck is the nightmare house?" We all soon found out.

The house was about a mile north on Forker Road. E94 had just passed the station on their way to the fire. We were glad they'd be first on the scene and take command. As we headed north, I started getting into my self-contained breathing apparatus (SCBA) and turned to Gabe, telling him, "Pack up!" The rear passenger compartment of our engine has three SCBAs, one built into each seat. This allows us to don our SCBAs before arriving on the scene. It sounds easier than it is, but it is doable, even when you're bouncing down the road in a four-wheel drive firetruck that rides like a buckboard.

When we arrived on the scene, the house was one incredible fireball. A half hour ago, it was a two-story wood-framed home. All we could see now was fire with dark outlines of the front gabled eaves and the porch's pickets and railings. We could hear it roaring and popping as we pulled up. Pitch-black heavy smoke shot hundreds of feet into the air, and we could feel the tremendous heat from the road over 100 feet away. Luckily, the forest surrounding the house was green. If it had been August, the house fire would have started a wildland fire that would have burned for a week.

The house sat behind a six-foot wooden fence surrounding a single acre bordering Forker Road. To the left of the house was a four-car garage. The right side of the garage and some of its contents were also on fire. A tree-and brush-studded creek ran alongside Forker Road in the front yard, so access to the house could only be made by going down the driveway in front of the garage. Our initial assignment was to help E94's crew advance a 2 ½-inch alleyway hose lay to the house. Once this was done, we would then attach a gated wye and a pair of 100-foot attack lines that would be used to extinguish the fire. That was the plan anyway. But the reality was that the driveway and front yard were both filled with parked vehicles and assorted refuse, much of it on fire, spewing black smoke and green, yellow, and blue flames. Car tires and what we guessed were small propane tanks were blowing up with the sound of canons that reverberated in our chests. It felt, sounded, and smelled like we were in the middle of a battle.

All this mayhem was going on while we were trying to position 200 feet of hose through a maze of parked cars and debris. Because of the smoke, we were all wearing structural turnouts and SCBAs, about 50 pounds of gear, and trying to drag charged hoselines. A 100-foot charged 2 1/2-inch hoseline weighs over 250 pounds, and every 100 feet of charged 1 3/4 hoseline weighs over 90 pounds. There is no easy way to do this work, especially when trying to weave in and out of twenty vehicles parked less than a foot apart and surrounded by other junk.

The house was a total loss. Consequently, we didn't waste water on the house and turned our full attention to the burning garage, cars, and refuse. In Command of the fire was Chief Mike Van Heal. He made his intentions clear by announcing over the radio, "We are *not* going to lose the garage!" To further make his point, he stood in the yard, pointed to a large truck, and said, "Do not let the fire reach this truck!" We had our marching orders.

As our fire attack progressed, Whitey and I took one of the attack lines and headed for the back of the garage. It was on fire, and we had to climb over a five-foot cedar fence to get to it. As we weaved our way through the maze of cars and refuse, we discovered engines, tires, wheels, and car parts everywhere, all creating obstacles and trip hazards. Our hoseline was getting caught with every zig or zag we made. The sound of the house fire about 50 feet to our right was a mix of roars, crackles, pops, collapsing lumber, and small explosions. Fire and noise were all around us. When we initially hit the burning debris with water, it would billow black smoke. The fire would then flare up. We kept moving toward the garage, knowing that if we diverted to extinguish the junk and debris, the garage would soon be fully involved.

As we approached the fence with Whitey handling the nozzle, I was holding onto his shoulder and watching the 40-foot brick chimney of the house that was to our right. I yelled to him, "If that chimney starts to fall, I'll yank hard on your shoulder. Drop the nozzle and run for cover." The chimney never fell and ended up being the only remaining part of the house.

When we reached the fence, we were overheated and fatigued. We stacked some yard debris next to the fence and labored over it one at a time. We sprayed the back and interior of the garage with 125 gallons per minute of water. Ten minutes later, our air bottles signaled we were getting low on air. I informed Command over the radio that we needed to cycle out and refill our air bottles. We struggled back over the fence, leaving our hoseline for our relief crew heading straight to rehab.

When we returned to the road, Lieutenant Steve Tevlin, our EMS coordinator, had rehab set up and welcomed us with his ever-present smile. We doffed our SCBAs and turnout coats and grabbed several bottles of water. We were both soaked with sweat and overheated. Turnouts are designed to keep the heat of a fire away from our bodies, which means any heat we generate while working can't escape. Our faces were beet red, and our hearts were racing. While we rested, Steve took repeated measurements of our heart rates and blood pressures and wouldn't let us return for another assignment until our vitals had returned to normal. It was about 20 minutes before we donned our gear with fresh air bottles and returned to work.

In the meantime, Captain Don had been working an attack line with Gabe. I had lost all contact with him, so I asked him to tell us in his own words what transpired.

The minute we got our eyes on this fire, we knew it would take a while to extinguish. I don't think we had ever seen this much fire in such a small space. The attack strategy was defensive, to contain the fire and keep it from spreading to nearby trees. Firefighters sometimes refer to this as 'keeping it in the box' or drawing a box around the containment area and keeping the fire inside that box.

The initial few minutes on the scene of a structure fire can be described as chaotic at best. All personnel move urgently and purposefully, doing their best to deploy attack lines and stop the destructive fire quickly. This was the case on this fire as well. As we arrived in E96, Command assigned us the task of helping establish the attack lines off E94. This proved challenging at best because of the amount of "stuff" piled against and in front of the garage, which impeded our path to the burning house.

Running on adrenaline, wholly focused on our task of quickly establishing the water lines that would stop this fire, we blocked out the distractions of the hungry, consuming flames and periodic explosions. But, at some point, I caught a glimpse out of the corner of my eye of a woman standing alone. She had black soot on her face, and the hair on her head was singed. This was the first time

I or anybody else noticed her. Where did she come from? Why hadn't we seen her earlier? Was she in the house when it was on fire? I stopped what I was doing, went over to her, and asked if she was OK. She told me how she was asleep on the couch in her living room when the fire started, adding, "Thankfully, my dog woke me up, and I was able to get out." She then described how her dog was barking excessively and climbing on her as she slept on the couch. Turns out, by the time the dog woke her, the house was already full of fire. I was concerned she had inhaled smoke and hot gases. So, I walked her to a safe place, the tailboard of E96, and requested a medic from one of the other crews on the scene check her out.

Now that the homeowner was cared for, it was time to return to work on those attack lines. The fire had extended to the garage next to the house. Crews were working hard to gain access to the garage and expose the fire so we could knock it down with our attack line.

Our other important objective was to keep the fire from spreading to the "stuff" in front of the garage. I keep calling it stuff because I can't recall exactly what it consisted of, only that there was a lot of it! Our overall objective was to stop the fire at the garage and not let it extend to the debris. The last thing we wanted was for this intense fire to gain all this added fuel! Thankfully, with the help of many firefighters, these objectives were accomplished after many intense, laborious hours.

In the end, this fire caused a lot of destruction. But thankfully, it turned out that Beverly, the homeowner, was fine and didn't need to be transported by ambulance to the hospital. Good thing her dog woke her up, or the outcome would have been much worse.

While those of us on E96 were on the attack lines, a critical challenge on this fire was creating a sufficient water supply. That responsibility fell on Gary and Jon.

Gary and Jon had rolled out of the station in WT96 right behind E96. As is customary, when they arrived on the scene, they fed a three-inch hoseline into E94, providing a 2,500-gallon reservoir for E94's attack lines. However, Engine 91 (E91) had arrived from the north and was attacking the fire on the property's north and west sides. They also needed a water supply. Even though each engine carries 750 gallons of water, they have a pump and multiple hoselines that can throw 250 gallons per minute on a fire. That's only three minutes of water from their water tank and an additional five minutes of water if they took all of WT96's 2,500 gallons. Therefore, the attack crews needed to manage their water use, and someone needed to make sure more water arrived quickly and constantly. That responsibility became Gary's problem when he was assigned the job of water supply. I'll let Gary tell you about his recollections of the fire.

Scanning the page, I noted that the address was close to my home, elevating the purposeful chaos defining my transformation from civilian to firefighter.

I had been cooking dinner; meals and calls collide more often than we would like. I gave rushed guidance on what needed to be done to complete the meal, one I probably would never see.

As I drove towards the firehouse, I rounded the corner from the county road onto Forker, recognizing the fire though it was buried in the trees. The flames were 20 feet above the 80-foot-tall pines. I could only mutter to no one, "Holy Shit." It was a fire that most of us only saw once in our careers.

It was a house I knew well, driving by it multiple times a week. One could not miss the eclectic collection of goods that filled virtually every inch of the property. It looked like a yard sale had reproduced multiple times. I always viewed this house as a potential nightmare for access and unknown hazards.

Unconsciously, I found myself in the wrong lane to further distance myself from flames roaring 30 feet from the road. It also led me to more than "observe the speed limit," thinking somewhat seriously that the fire would melt parts of my car.

I arrived at the station to find the engine ready to roll. I ran into the turnout bay where Dan and Jon were gearing up. As he headed to the truck bay, I told Dan, 'It's the Nightmare House. We'll bring the tender. You are going to need water!" What an understatement.

I stepped into my turnouts and prepared my gear and psyche for what lay ahead. We boarded the tender and headed for the fire, with Jon driving.

Arriving on the scene as the first tender, the Incident Commander assigned me the task of Water Supply Officer. Jon would spend the night in the tender, shuttling much-needed water to the fire.

Eventually, we would have seven tenders and two different fill stations on opposite sides of the fire. On the scene, two engines were pumping 250 gallons a minute, going through an average tender every 12 minutes. It was a full plate managing this very active water supply group. We delivered over 110,000 gallons of water that night and around 20,000 more over the next few days.

The engines and the water supply group worked on Forker Road, about 15 feet above the property. The fire played out like a theater in front of us. I was amazed by the height and breadth of this fire. It also exhibited quite a pallet of colors from the various materials burning in the yard and house.

Rain fell later that night, but it served little to influence the fire other than to keep it out of the trees. In a moment of quiet, I glanced across the road and noticed that despite the rain, the woods were full of onlookers who had hiked in to witness this nightmare unfold.

One of the reasons the house burned with such intensity was that the homeowners were hoarders. One of the owners' sons later told the press that his parents hoarded "everything you can imagine… including wood, materials, and pets like the people featured on the TV show *Hoarders*." He also said he believed the home hasn't had running water in a long time. Neighbors described the interior of the house as packed with stuff. Our problem was that everything was combustible: paper, magazines, furniture, boxes, and more.

The house had so much fuel contained in such a confined space that when it caught fire, it burned like a road flare. We eventually used over 100,000 gallons of water during the three days it took to fully extinguish the fire. In addition, the amount of fuel presented by over twenty parked vehicles and an unknown mass of refuse presented numerous challenges for us. For years, Gary had driven by that house every day and knew of the contents of the house and yard. He also knew that if it someday caught fire, it would be a nightmare to stop. He was right.

Chief Van Heal later described this fire as a "career fire." He told us we'd probably never again be on a structure fire that burned as hot. Mike retired a few years ago, and he's been right so far. But I'm not sure we won't see another fire bigger and hotter than this one. All the volunteers at our station live in the community, and most days we drive by houses and properties that present similar, or worse, nightmare scenarios. We often go into these properties on medical calls or smoke investigations. Having seen the inside and outside of the houses and properties, we all dread what we know is inevitable. Someday, for some reason, we'll be back wearing turnouts and SCBAs. It's not something we look forward to, but it's what we signed up for.

Chapter 5

How Did I Get Here?

My dad was a career firefighter for 20 years in Providence, Rhode Island. He was born on August 1, 1921, and died of lung cancer 59 years later, on December 23, 1980.

I sat with Dad in his hospital room during his last night. I was waiting for him to take his last breath. The cancer in his lungs and esophagus had transformed his body and mind into someone I no longer recognized, could no longer talk with, and no longer reach. I could only watch him die. As I sat through the night, stuck with only my thoughts, I could remember only two times when he spoke about his experiences as a firefighter. The first instance was when I was in high school. We were looking at some old photographs of us. In one of the pictures, I stood next to him on the porch of an old, one-room lake cabin my parents had rented for a rare two-week summer vacation. When the picture was taken, I was four years old. He was thirty-eight. I looked at the picture and commented that he was much heavier back then. He told me he lost the extra weight soon after that picture was taken. He had been working on a structure fire and found himself lying in the dark on the floor of a smoke-filled room. He was on the floor because he was trying to find air to breathe. He didn't think he was going to survive. Fortunately, he did crawl out of the building. He said the extra 50 pounds of body weight almost killed him, and he decided it was time to lose it. He was never that heavy again.

The second time he mentioned something about his firefighting experiences was when I asked him why he retired from the fire department. I don't know when I asked the question, but it was probably not long after our conversation about his weight, sometime in the early 1970s.

He retired in the late 1960s when there was considerable social unrest in South Providence. It was especially bad during the hot and humid summer months of July and August. Consequently, his fire station regularly responded to structure fires purposely lit in abandoned houses in and around the projects of South Providence. Whenever the firefighters arrived to fight the fires, people from the neighborhood would throw rocks and bottles at the firefighters, yelling, "Let it burn!" He said he retired because he just couldn't put up with it anymore. I can't say that I blame him. My sister Mickey believes Dad retired because he was unhappy with the leadership in the Department. Perhaps the two issues were related. We'll never know.

My dad joined the Providence Fire Department in the mid-1940s, a short while after he returned to Providence from having served in WWII at places like Normandy and Belgium (he was at the well-known Battle of the Bulge). Not surprisingly, Dad never spoke of his military service either. However, he once told me the large scar on his right shoulder was from being stabbed with a bayonet by a German soldier. I later learned the scar was from surgery to repair a dislocated shoulder suffered while playing high school football. I sometimes think of him when my right shoulder aches or I try to throw a ball for our dog Tyson. In 1991, I dislocated my shoulder in a "high side" motorcycle crash at Sears Point raceway. I was racing my 250 cc Honda Grand Prix bike in the Formula 1 class and grabbed too much throttle while coming out of a first-gear chicane. I never had the surgery my dad had, but I should have. It was an anterior-inferior dislocation, which has popped out of few times over the years. Because of the injury, I can no longer throw a ball with any speed or distance, and it aches anytime the barometric pressure drops. My dad never complained of his shoulder aching, but even post-surgery, he also never recovered his ability to throw. He had been an all-star shortstop in high school before his injury. But, just like me, after the injury, he could hardly throw a ball from short to first base. I was a center fielder in high school with a powerful throwing arm. Years after my accident, I can't throw anything more than 30 feet. Like father, like son.

That old story about his scar was not his only fib about an injury. Dad was missing the distal half of his right ring finger. When I was a child, he told me he lost the tip of his finger when the wheel of a fire truck ran over it. I later discovered the truth: he lost it while running a die press making bubble gum wrappers in a factory. It was perhaps a bit ironic that when I was in my teens, I worked a summer job in a local factory using a die press, much like the one that took off a part of his finger. I thought about him losing the end of his finger probably every night I worked in that factory. Perhaps that thought of him losing part of his finger helped me keep all of mine.

My eldest sister, Mickey, recently told me what she remembered of Dad's firefighting career. I'll let her tell you in her own words.

> Dad retired after 20 years of service because he was frustrated with the leadership above him. He had taken the test for a promotion a few times but couldn't pass it. Mom helped him study, but he still struggled. He was naturally intelligent, artistic, and capable of almost anything but struggled in school. He probably had a learning disability. He worked at two stations I know of and rotated to others nearby as a sub. I believe he moved to the Allens Ave. station after Broad St..
>
> I saw him at a fire on Broad St. once, and he was at the top of the ladder with all his equipment on and hosing the flames from a large window. Before I recognized him, I told a friend I wouldn't want to be that fireman.
>
> He had other jobs while working at the fire department. He did house painting, wallpapering, cement work, and cab driving. When he bought his cab, he struggled with drivers he hired when he had to work at the fire department.

Other than what I've presented here, I can't remember much else about my dad's career as a firefighter. I sometimes visited him at the fire station and distinctly remember the Broad St. station in South Providence. The station had two levels. The first floor consisted of the truck bay and kitchen area, while the second floor was sleeping quarters. I remember they had beautiful brass firepoles they would slide down for an alarm. I always wanted to try sliding down one of those poles, but I wasn't brave enough to ask if I could. The pole was just out of my reach, and I would have had to leap for it. If I missed it, it probably would have hurt a lot. I'm unsure if they use those brass poles anymore, but it still sounds fun.

I also have clear memories of climbing all over the engines and ladder trucks at Broad Street station. The ladder truck had a tiller on the back, and I would sit up there and pretend I could turn the enormous steering wheel. It was great fun. I also remember listening and watching the crew sitting in the truck bay in white tee shirts and khaki pants, smoking cigarettes, drinking coffee, and arguing about sports and politics. They mostly were Irishmen like my dad and could argue forever.

It's little wonder my dad always had a cigarette between his fingers and a cup of coffee in his hand. They were the first things he picked up in the morning and the last he put down before bed. Perhaps it was something his generation picked up in the military and carried with them to the firehouses. There was always second-hand smoke and the smell of instant coffee at home when he was there. Luckily, I never picked up the smoking habit, but I was a regular coffee drinker by the time I graduated from high school, just not the instant stuff he and the boys at the station drank.

Oddly enough, I never thought I should or would become a firefighter. Dad never hinted about it, either. Perhaps it was because he never graduated from high school and always struggled to provide for us like he wanted. Career firefighters in Providence didn't receive anywhere near the pay and benefits of today's career firefighters. I'm pretty sure Dad was making about $5,000 per year in the late '60s. Adjusting for inflation, that's equivalent to about $43,000 per year in 2022, not much to support a wife, four kids, and a mortgage. Understandably, Dad was adamant that I and my three older siblings get a college education. He wanted us to "have a better chance at a good life." There were mixed results on the issue of college, but the McCann kids have all prospered.

When I left our home in Providence and headed off to college, I quickly learned that I loved college. Before I was done, I earned a Bachelor of Science in Physical Education, a Master of Arts in Ergonomics, and a Doctorate in Physiology. These degrees eventually led to my accepting a university position as an Assistant Professor in 1992, teaching anatomy and physiology in Spokane, WA, and perhaps, inevitably, becoming a volunteer firefighter and emergency medical technician (EMT) in SCFD9. So, in a very round-a-bout way, college led me back to hanging out at the local fire station.

Not surprisingly, the crew at Station 96 often sits around drinking coffee and discussing recent events, just like the guys in my dad's station. When we do it, it's usually after training, which we do every Tuesday night. But unlike my dad's crew, we're not all Irish, none of us smoke, and white tee shirts and khakis are never the day's uniform. So, I guess we're a new variation of the old guard.

Of course, the probability of coming to Spokane to be a university professor and, in the process, becoming a Lieutenant in a rural volunteer fire station is probably low. So, let me explain how it happened. I'll try to be brief.

When I arrived in Spokane in the fall of 1992, I met Dr. Dick Green, a colleague in my department who was also hired that fall. Dick and his wife, Sue Anderson, had just moved to Spokane and bought a house in town. However, their intention was, like mine, to buy some land and build a new home. Within a year of moving to Spokane, they found their 30-acre dream property and, the following summer started building a beautiful house overlooking the City of Spokane Valley. I had come to Spokane straight out of graduate school, and like most graduate students, I had a negative net worth. Therefore, during my first year in Spokane, I rented a small duplex and saved enough for a down payment on a starter home on the west side of town. I planned on spending a year or two saving money and looking for my dream property.

When I was in Spokane to interview for the university position during the summer of 1992, I rented a car and drove through the Foothills area on an afternoon sightseeing trip to Mount Spokane. I was so impressed by the beauty of the Foothills that I decided this was where I'd live if I got the job. So, after visiting Dick and Sue numerous times in their new rural home, which happened to be in the Foothills, I started looking for a similar property. It took me over two years, but I finally found a parcel about a mile from Dick and Sue on Forker Ridge. It was 17 acres and had a spectacular southern view of the Spokane Valley. Nothing was on the parcel except timber, brush, and wildlife. It was perfect.

The first few challenges in moving to the property were building a road into the property, bringing in underground power, and putting in a septic tank and drain field. All new tasks for a city boy, but Dick and Sue coached me through it.

I bought a 20-year-old 19-foot Terry travel trailer, had it towed to the property, and lived in it for the next two years. One morning that first summer, I drove down my new driveway and met a large black bear sitting in the switchback. I named my private road Black Bear Lane. It was official; I had become a country boy.

At the time, the housing market in Spokane could have been better, so when I moved to my new travel trailer on the new property, I rented out my home in town. A year later, the market improved, and I sold the house to my renter, using the small profit to pay for drilling a well. I made enough money selling the house to drill 350 feet. They found water at 320 feet, 10 gallons per minute. I was ecstatic. I was soon ready to build a home.

More relevant to my story here, Dick had joined SCFD9 as a volunteer firefighter/EMT when he and Sue moved to the Foothills. When he discovered my dad was a firefighter, Dick suggested I join. I thought it was a great idea. Growing up in Providence, I had no idea that volunteer firefighters still existed, so the opportunity sounded like a bonus to my living in the country. It was a chance to finally know a bit more about what my dad's life as a firefighter might have been like.

In the summer of 1996, I enrolled in SCFD9's Firefighter Academy and EMT courses. We trained every Wednesday night from 6 to 10 PM and all day Saturday. I attended fire school for the first three months and then three months of EMT school. In addition, I completed classroom and practical classes to qualify to drive and operate the pumps and equipment on our three fire trucks. I also completed specific courses for wildland fires. I enjoyed all of it and finally became a fully qualified volunteer Firefighter/EMT in the fall of 1996. I was 41 years old.

In 1996, we had about 20 volunteer firefighters at Station 96. A few of them were charter members of the station, meaning they were part of the first crew to staff Station 96. The station was formed in the early 70s when SCFD9 agreed to annex the Foothills area and build its sixth station: Station 96. The creation of Station 96 was ultimately a consequence of a local home burning down. My understanding is that a couple of neighbors who were farmers and owned water trucks drove to the house and tried to put the fire out. They almost succeeded but ran out of water because they could only get one of their two trucks to start. Knowing they needed additional help extinguishing the fire, they phoned the two nearest fire districts for assistance. However, both districts had policies that prevented them from leaving their respective districts to fight fires. Consequently, the home burned to the ground. The Foothills Association then created a group to begin annexation discussions with SCFD9, which eventually led to annexing the Foothills area and creating Station 96.

When I joined Station 96, the volunteers were an eclectic group. They were farmers, truck drivers, machinists, construction workers, salesmen, a local pastor, and more. Three or four younger guys were volunteering, hoping to become career firefighters someday. A few of them eventually did. A few, like Dick and myself, were recent arrivals in the Foothills who thought volunteering was a great way to serve the community.

When I joined, almost all the volunteers at the station had grown up in the Foothills area. They all knew each other and each other's families. Some were related. For example, in cases like the Atwood and Shearer families, father and son were volunteers serving simultaneously.

One of the funny things I soon discovered when I became a volunteer was that with such a local group, it was more common than not that addresses were seldom used to describe where an event occurred. Often, locations were described as "Over at the old Wruble place…" or "Just south of Peterson's field…". If you asked for a road name, you might get, "Oh, I don't know, it didn't have a name for years, but then they gave it a name back when that Macmahan fella built a big fancy home." It drove me crazy back then but makes me smile now. It still happens occasionally with conversations between Don and Gary, who grew up about a mile from the fire station. Sometimes, I even hear myself doing it.

My schedule while working at the university was such that I often worked at home. Consequently, I was usually available to respond to most of our calls. But things have improved in the last three years since retiring in 2020. In 2021, our station had 167 emergency calls, and I responded to 84% of them. Going to those calls was sometimes the best part of my day. Sometimes, it was the most difficult. But overall, it has become more personally rewarding than I ever imagined. Volunteering has also given me something to look forward to daily, and Tuesday night training drills have become a significant part of my social life. Some guys refer to volunteering as "man scouts" because we dress up in uniforms and go on adventures. That description is not far from the truth.

Twenty-six years after joining Station 96, I am 68 years old and the oldest firefighter at the station. Only Captain Don, who first joined when he was 16, has been here longer. He is now 67. I have seen many volunteers come and go over the years. Some stayed for decades; others lasted a year or two. We now have just six active volunteers at Station 96: a small crew, to say the least, and one that will likely get smaller even as our call volume gets larger. Don, Gary, and I are in our sixties, and the other guys average over forty years old.

As the years pass, I'm reluctantly thinking more and more about retiring. We have about 130 active firefighters in SCFD9. Approximately 65% are salaried career firefighters, and the rest are volunteers. I'm not positive, but I think I am the oldest active firefighter in the fire district. I'm not sure what to think about that!

So that's how I got here. It wasn't planned, and looking back on it, it was, perhaps, inevitable. But I'm sure leaving will be hard. Maybe next year should be my last. Or perhaps I can make it to seventy. Who knows? Every day is an adventure when you're a firefighter. It's hard to give that up.

Chapter 6

I Couldn't Do That.
Could You Do That?
How Can They Do That?
Who Are Those Guys?

Butch Cassidy (played by Paul Newman) asked the questions in the title of this chapter on the silver screen back in 1969 during the movie *Butch Cassidy and the Sundance Kid.* His questions went unanswered even though Butch asked them repeatedly, each time with an increasing sense of bewilderment. I thought I'd answer his questions regarding my guys at Station 96. I've written very little about them; you should know them better. They deserve that, at the very least.

I interviewed each volunteer while we sipped a beverage of their choosing. This chapter summarizes those interviews to help you understand who they are and why they serve. During each interview, I asked them 16 questions. The experience was sometimes surprising, fun, and always enlightening. I interviewed Captain Don Shearer, Training Lieutenant Gary Woollett, Logistics Lieutenant Jon Amend, Firefighter/EMT Matt Olinger, retired Firefighter/EMT Mark Friendshuh, and Firefighter/EMT Gavin Duffey. The group (including myself) ranges from 38 to 68 years of age. It is an eclectic group.

Lieutenant Gary and I have retired from our professional careers. Gary retired after 32 years as an aluminum industry process/software engineer. I retired after 28 years as a Professor of Physiology at a local Liberal Arts university. The rest of the crew still work full-time. Captain Don is the sole proprietor of a small company he purchased in 2014. His company specializes in interior and exterior lighting for residential homes and small businesses. Before buying the business, Don served as a pastor in a local church for 11 years. Lieutenant Jon is currently the manager of a local bike shop in Spokane. He also has worked as a contract wildland firefighter for many years. Matt is a journeyman pipefitter in Spokane. Mark recently began working as a realtor. Before that, he was a stay-at-home dad for 15 years after having retired from being a corporate lawyer. Gavin is the Chief Deputy US Marshall in the Eastern District of Washington State. All of us are married, and everyone except me has children. Some guys have kids attending local public schools, while others have adult children who have moved out of the area.

Each volunteer joined the station under different circumstances, but their reasons were similar. They all highly valued serving their community and thought volunteering might be interesting, fun, and exciting. None thought it would be a stepping stone to becoming a career firefighter. However, several have enjoyed volunteering in the fire service so much that they have, at one time or another, considered pursuing a career in the fire service.

Captain Don was 16 years old when he joined Station 96. The station had been established a year or so earlier, and he: "Wanted to be a part of it." It was a family affair for Don because his dad, Carl, was a charter member of the station. Many years later, Don's son Chris also joined.

Lieutenant Gary also grew up in the foothills and knew Don in those early years. Gary's father, Sid, was a charter member of Station 96. However, Gary didn't join until he was 46 years old. And, even though there were others in Gary's extended circle of family and friends who were career firefighters, he never considered firefighting a possible career back then. However, after 21 years of volunteering, Gary admits that "firefighting would have been a hell of a good job."

I've written about Gary's decision to join the station in another chapter (see *Empathy and Compassion*), so I'll not repeat that story here. However, Gary told me his joining was primarily motivated by his wife, Theresa, and their son, Isaac. The three of them joined Station 96 in 2002. Theresa and Isaac both served for about five years before retiring.

Jon has been with us for about 16 years. He grew up in the Foothills and had several family members living on 200 acres of land a few miles west of Station 96. After finishing college and getting married, he and his wife, Krista, built their new home on 20 acres of what we jokingly call the "Amend compound." For several years, Jon worked as a wildland contractor with his brother Joe. Jon told me that joining the Station "seemed like the right thing to do." None of his immediate family had ever volunteered at Station 96. Still, his dad was a medic in the army, and his grandfather, a physician, served as Spokane County's Medical Examiner for decades. Although Jon never planned or foresaw that he would also become an EMT as part of joining the station, he now loves responding to medical calls just as much as responding to wildland fires.

Matt and Mark joined Station 96 eight and six years ago, respectively. While Matt was growing up, a cousin and two uncles served at Station 96. As a youngster, Matt spent considerable time listening to them on the home radio scanner as they responded to calls. Matt still considers his uncles and cousins heroes of the community. When Matt and his wife, Amanda, bought his grandmother's house across the street from the fire station, it was, in Matt's words, inevitable that he become a member of the station.

Mark and his family moved to the Foothills about 16 years ago. He was a stay-at-home dad when he joined Station 96 ten years later. His wife, Sandra, works as a Physician in Spokane. At the early age of 16, Mark had been a volunteer wildland firefighter with the Buffalo Gap Volunteer Fire Department in South Dakota. Mark's dad, Gary, was a ranch owner in South Dakota and a long-time volunteer, so it was only natural Mark joined when he was old enough. Mark told me that his experiences fighting wildland fires gave him a deep appreciation of the value of servicing as a local volunteer. When he and his family settled into the Foothills near Station 96, joining up seemed the right thing to do. He explained it to me this way, "It's what you did as part of the community, and I loved it. I always loved when the pager would go off. It's like being on a sports team with the trust, belonging, and camaraderie established among the firefighters."

Gavin joined our group about four years ago. He was 42. He moved to the Foothills when he accepted the Chief Deputy US Marshall position for the Easter District of Washington. Gavin also has years of combat experience working in air resource management for the Air Force in Afghanistan. That experience spurred his interest in learning more about the use of air support in wildland firefighting. His primary reason for joining Station 96 was to altruistically give back to the community, particularly by protecting it from wildfires.

Overall, the volunteers at Station 96 joined because they recognized the value of community service. This recognition was partially born from witnessing the benefit of others in their family, friends, and the community. They all agreed that having others model community service helped instill their desire to serve.

Throughout my life, I have often realized that witnessing an activity from the outside and participating in that activity later in life can sometimes reveal that all is not necessarily as I anticipated. In other words, being a professor, parent, or firefighter can be different from what one's earlier observations might have suggested. Consequently, after discovering why my colleagues joined Station 96, I asked them what they liked best about volunteering and what they thought was the toughest part.

Generally, the best parts of volunteering followed two themes. One theme was how much everyone enjoyed being part of the crew. Everyone enjoys the time we spend together, whether on calls helping others in the community or working at the station doing the training that makes us better at what we do. The mix of service, teamwork, and personal growth all rolled into one makes volunteering worthwhile. Everyone repeatedly expressed their commitment to both the community and the station. They also recognized that when you live through challenging situations, like those described in this book, deep bonds form: bonds that become very meaningful. For example, they told me the most challenging part of volunteering has been seeing and experiencing the tragedy, loss, and sorrow that is part of helping people when they need it most. Their interviews revealed that they were most affected by calls involving children and young adults. Several individuals commented that a particular call involving a child made them think of their children, forcing them to wonder how they would be affected if this happened to them. They all admit that getting past their reaction to seeing the pain and loss of others can be very difficult and stressful. Yet, they also believe that stress can be eased by the support of their teammates, even if those teammates were not on that particular call.

Despite the ongoing challenges of dealing with tragedy and stress regularly, everyone expressed they would do it again in a heartbeat. They also were adamant they would recommend volunteering to others. However, everyone qualified this perspective by acknowledging that not everyone is "cut out" or "well suited" to do this type of work. When pressed further, they expressed that volunteers needed more than a willingness to serve others. They also needed humility, patience, and a deep desire and ability to learn. They believe an excellent volunteer must be able to accept and value critical analyses of their work. Several also mentioned that volunteers needed self-confidence and had to be able to focus and function under pressure in chaotic situations. They also emphasized the need for volunteers to have a desire and ability to learn from past mistakes.

When I asked each volunteer what specific personal advice they would give to a new volunteer, their responses included being open to learning new skills, showing up for everything they can, always asking for help, being willing to do whatever needs to be done, slowing down and staying calm, and being careful not to put their volunteer responsibility ahead of their commitment to their family. All of it sounded like good advice to me.

Not surprisingly, none had any regrets about volunteering. Some wished they had joined earlier, while others wished the training earlier in their careers was as good as it is now. But overall, they wouldn't change anything. When I asked them what they felt was the most rewarding part of volunteering, they mostly returned to those things they enjoyed about it, such as the camaraderie within the station and the feeling of being a part of an experienced and successful team.

As time passed since joining Station 96, I have increasingly sensed that we all have been changed by the work we do as volunteers. How could we not be? But I wondered whether my colleagues shared my view. So, I asked them: Has volunteering changed you?

Most answered this question by discussing their growth as a firefighter and EMT. They expressed how they now had a greater appreciation of the job and felt their skills and experience made them much better at doing the work. But they struggled to answer when I asked them if they thought it affected who they have become rather than what they can do. One or two were unsure if they had changed. But a few did believe they had greater compassion and empathy for the people they serve. I sensed they just hadn't thought about it before. But when asked directly to reflect on the question, most agreed that volunteering had increased their compassion and empathy, especially for those they didn't know and might never see again.

Near the end of each interview, I brought the discussion full circle by asking if the reasons they continue to serve are different than their original reasons for joining. As you might remember, the group's reasons for joining were that they wanted to serve their community and thought it might be interesting, fun, and exciting. These reasons have remained throughout their careers. However, their primary reason for staying had migrated away from the fun and excitement and shifted towards their desire and commitment to serve the community. Notably, after years of serving the community, they also spoke equally of their growing desire to serve Station 96. We have become a "band of brothers" with an identity that deserves care and commitment.

Chapter 7

Blue Scrubs and Comfortable Walking Shoes

It was a typical cold mid-October Friday morning. It was pitch dark when my wife, Karie, left home for work at 5:30 AM. She wore her usual attire, blue scrubs and comfortable walking shoes.

After she kissed me goodbye and headed to the garage, I reached for my phone and turned off the "do not disturb" function. I do this because she might need me during her 35-minute drive to the hospital. For example, on a cold, snowy winter's morning not too long ago, she called minutes after leaving the house because she was stuck in the snow on our unplowed county road. She needed me to pull her out of the ditch with our pickup. On another occasion, she called me from Moffat Road after hitting a deer with her car. She was in tears, asking if I would come quickly to relieve the injured deer's misery. But, thankfully, on this particular Friday morning in October, as on most mornings, she made it to work without a problem.

An hour later, at 6:30 AM, my pager went off. It was a 46D. The 46 code indicates a motor vehicle accident (MVA), and the D, or delta code, indicates possible life-threatening injuries.

I quickly sent my "On my way!" text to our volunteer group, grabbed my SCFD9 jacket, and headed for our shop. Before I reached it, incoming texts indicated Captain Don was responding to the station, and Gary was responding POV to the scene. I climbed in our Polaris RZR side-by-side, fired it up, and headed down the hill. The ride to the station is 1.25 miles through the woods. It starts with a two-track trail that takes me down a steep grade of tight twists and turns through heavy timber. At the bottom is a shallow creek crossing. I crossed the creek with a large splash and roared up the other side, racing along a two-track path that dumped me out on the dirt and gravel public right-of-way. From the creek crossing to the station is uphill with abrupt rises that always get the RZR airborne. There are also sharp dips that bottom out the suspension if I don't lift off the throttle at just the right time. The end of the right-of-way rises steeply as it joins the west end of a gravel road that leads to the station. Because it's cold and pitch dark, I'm thankful I'm in the RZR and not still riding my old Kawasaki dirt bike.

When I arrived at the station, I climbed out of the RZR, pulled off my helmet and gloves, and punched in the entry code to the station door. As I entered the turnout room, I dumped my gloves and helmet, grabbed my SCFD9 hat, and pushed through the entrance to the truck bay. The bay was dark and quiet. I had seen Don's pickup parked outside the station, so I knew he'd be sitting in the brush truck waiting for me.

While it takes me about four minutes to get from my house to the station, Don can make it in two or three minutes. While waiting for me, he used the time to get in the brush truck, pinpoint the location of the call on the truck's automated vehicle location device (AVL), plan our route, and see what other resources were on the call. I slid into the driver's seat, started the truck, hit the garage door opener, and off we went, lights and sirens.

Don called Dispatch on the radio and told them we were responding. The response from Dispatch (what we call "the short") was that we had one car off the side of the driveway with one patient. Engine 94 and an AMR unit (American Medical Response ambulance) were also responding. Because the location of the call was close, we knew we'd be first on-scene. Don would be Incident Command (IC), and I would have patient care. About three minutes after leaving the station, we pulled into a long gravel driveway that led to three homes.

Don is friends with one of the families living along this driveway. He recognized a man pointing to an SUV parked off on the side of the driveway and down a small embankment. The car had its lights on and was lodged against a deer fence surrounding a small orchard.

We parked just past the SUV to give E94 and the AMR unit room to park when they arrived. I grabbed the EMS bag, and Don called Dispatch on his portable radio to update them that we were on the scene. In the dim morning light, I could see an elderly couple standing beside the SUV. My first thought was one of relief because they both seemed uninjured. But as I approached, I saw the gentleman's arm around the woman's shoulder. She was crying as she looked up at me and pointed at the SUV. She quietly spoke two words, "She's gone." I kept moving towards the SUV.

Walking down the embankment, I saw that the car was still running and the driver's door was partly open. A middle-aged woman was hanging halfway out of the driver's door. She was motionless. Her torso and head were pinned between the fence and the side of the car. The fence was preventing the car from rolling farther down the embankment. Only her legs remained in the vehicle. In the dim light, I could see she was wearing blue scrubs. On her feet were comfortable white walking shoes. My first thought was that she must work at a hospital and had been on her way to work. I wondered if my wife knew her. I cleared my mind and got to work assessing her condition.

Her neck and face were purple and swollen. She was unresponsive. The fence was a wire field fence with four-inch square openings. Reaching my hand through the fence, I could barely reach one of her wrists. She had no radial pulse. As Don approached the car, I turned my head to face him, "Full arrest," I said. He immediately saw the situation and radioed Dispatch to upgrade the call to an extrication call.

I was frustrated because there was nothing else I could do. I considered returning to the brush truck to get our wire cutters to cut away the fence, but if I cut the fence, I knew the car would roll forward down the embankment and run over both me and her. Just then, I heard the engine and air brakes of E94 stop on the other side of the car.

Matt VonStuben was the first person off of E94 and joined me. He's also the Paramedic, so I gave him a patient update and turned patient care over to him. As he set down his ALS medical bag and LifePack 1500, he ordered his crew to see if they could shut off the car and stabilize it. He started pulling ECG leads and a blood pressure cuff from his gear and then realized, as I had, that we couldn't get to her through the fence. We were both quiet for a moment. She was gone, and there was nothing more we could have done. It was obvious to us she had been trapped for quite a while. Just then, her phone rang. It startled us both, and we saw it light up in her shirt pocket. Matt was able to get his fingers on it and pulled it through the fence. He held it out, and we both saw the call was from a contact she had labeled "Boss." Matt canceled the call and put it in his pocket. "I'll give this to Chief Bleaker," he said. Doug Bleaker was the Duty Chief for the day and had just arrived on the scene. I nodded in agreement. We looked at each other with nothing else to say.

More pieces of the incident started to come together from information Don had gathered from the elderly couple and neighbors. The victim's husband had left for work around 4:30 AM. The victim typically left at 5:30

AM. She probably was trapped for a least an hour before we arrived. The neighbor that Don recognized on our arrival was Mark. He had been first to see the car parked off the driveway from his kitchen window. It had its lights on, so he went out to investigate. When he saw the situation, he called 911. He and his wife, Anne, were close friends with the victim. The elderly couple standing by the car when we arrived lived just across the driveway. They were the victim's parents. I couldn't imagine what they all must have been feeling. Seeing something like that happen to strangers was mind-numbing. Seeing it happen to loved ones must have been crushing. How would they ever get these images out of their minds? The unfortunate truth is they won't.

Don had asked Mike to call the victim's husband. He suggested that Mike not let the husband go to the car until the extrication crew had removed her from the vehicle. However, the husband ran straight to the car when he arrived home. We could hear him wailing in anguish across the driveway. I had a brief urge to call my wife but put it out of my mind. Now was not the time, and this was certainly not the place. Besides, what would I say?

These types of calls are unimaginably tragic for family and friends. For volunteer firefighters who live in the community and often know the people involved, they are both frustrating and hard to forget. Don later told me he had gone to school with the victim but had not recognized her at the time of the call. On our drive back to the station, we discussed the frustration of being unable to help. No matter how much we train or how quickly we get to the scene, we can still be too late to make a difference.

A call like this also shows us that the space between the lives of the people in the community who call for help and the lives of those who race to provide that help can disappear instantly. On this call, the sight of blue scrubs and comfortable walking shoes was all it took for me.

Chapter 8

The Whipple Road Fire

Approximately 85% of wildland fires in the US are caused by human activity. These human-caused fires result from unattended campfires, escaped burn piles, equipment use (combines, tractors, etc.), discarded cigarettes, and various other activities, including arson. In 2015, we were getting more than our usual share of local arson fires.

On August 14, 2015, a warm, smoky, and windy Friday, the National Weather Service issued a Red Flag Warning for the Spokane area. Red Flag Warnings indicate warm temperatures, humidity below 20%, and strong winds are expected to produce a significantly increased risk of fire danger.

A little after 6:10 PM, my pager went off for a 14H. In Spokane County, a 14H results in a fire response that includes three brush trucks, three Type-1 structural engines, and two 3,000-gallon water tenders. In addition to these resources, several "overhead" resources respond to all 14H calls. The resources include the District's Duty Chief, known as the "20-Officer," along with various other officers from SCFD9 who perform different roles such as logistics, operations, air support, and public information liaison.

When the call went out for the Whipple Fire, Randy, the volunteer captain from Station 98, was driving their water tender (WT98) to transfer multiple loads of water from a fire hydrant located a couple of miles southwest of Station 96 to the 130,000-gallon cistern behind our station. Our cistern was down to about 30,000 gallons from fighting the Macmahan Fire on August 5 through the 9th.

Immediately after the alarm registered on our pagers and phones, several SCFD9 career stations staffed 24/7 with career firefighters began responding. Because Randy is from nearby Station 98, his water tender was also on the call. He had just filled up with water and was headed back to our cistern, so all he had to do was take a left turn and drive north about 1/2 mile to reach the fire. Randy has been with SCFD9 as a volunteer for 40-plus years, so responding to a brush fire was nothing new. However, Randy knew that being first on the scene in a water tender, rather than a brush or attack engine, gave him few options to fight the fire. So, although he was unsure about what he could achieve as the first unit on the scene, he was determined to make a positive impact.

As Randy drove to the fire, he saw the smoke column leaning over hard to the north. When he arrived on the scene, the fire was about one acre, spreading fast, and headed towards heavy timber at the north end of a 10-acre field. It was also spreading east and west toward neighboring homes. Randy immediately radioed Dispatch with a brief size-up and prepared to make his initial attack using one of the 1 3/4-inch hoselines on his tender.

The field on fire had been fallow for several years and contained plenty of crisp, dry grass and brush. It also was dotted with isolated small and medium-sized Ponderosa Pine. The northern end of the field was heavy timber and dropped down into a large draw that contains Moffat Road, numerous homes, and a few small farms. Randy began by putting out as much fire as he could on the southwest corner of the field. There was nothing else he could do until help arrived.

To Randy's relief, B94 soon arrived on the scene. The officer on B94 was Lieutenant Cody Traber, the same Cody Traber that Don transferred command to on the Macmahan Fire. Cody immediately took Command and directed his crew to make a mobile attack on the right flank of the fire. Cody's sizeup to Dispatch was that the wind-blown fire was now about three acres and heading for heavy timber.

When I arrived at Station 96 after my typical dirt bike ride through the woods, I was a couple of minutes behind Captain Don. I quickly donned my wildland gear and found Don sitting in B96. He arrived a minute or two before me and was making sure he knew where we were going, putting the truck radio on the correct channel, and listening to the size-up as WT98 and B94 arrived on the scene.

I climbed into the driver's seat, started the truck, and asked, "Left or right?" "Right," Don said. Usually, when I read my pager, I recognize the road name and know where we're going. I had no idea where Whipple Road was. Down the ramp we went, taking a sharp right and heading south on Forker Road. Don turned on the lights and sirens.

"Take Pleasant Prairie and then a right on Whipple. Whipple is just after Tracey," he said. He then told Dispatch over the radio we were responding.

Dispatch gave us the "short." B94 and WT98 were on the scene of a wind-driven three-acre field fire that was headed for structures and timber. The short from Dispatch got our attention and raised our heart rates. We were apparently in for a busy evening.

We were heading west on Pleasant Prairie Road, climbing the hill to the prairie. Soon we had our first view of the smoke column. Sure enough, we saw the heavy gray smoke leaning over to the north. When we arrived at the fire, Cody told us to do a mobile attack on the left flank.

A mobile attack is supposed to be done by slowly driving a brush or attack engine in the burned part of the field (called the black), paralleling and extinguishing the flank of the fire. This approach keeps the firefighters and their trucks relatively safe because the fire is moving away from them and has already consumed all the fuel in the black. Even if the wind reverses direction, the fire cannot turn and run at the firefighters. The attack requires that one firefighter drives slowly while the other uses the 200-foot reel-mounted 3/4 inch rubber-coated attack line to extinguish the fire. This is what B94 was doing on the right flank. Our problem was that the left flank was filled with brush, timber, and scattered basalt rocks. Randy had tried to extinguish this part of the field, but his reach was limited to 200 feet from the road. The fire was gaining momentum just north of Randy's reach, moving west and north.

To the west was a large stubble field and a residence. This meant our most effective attack would be from that unburnt stubble field. But by fighting fire from the unburned field, we would be fighting in the green, not the black. Fighting from the green is risky but can yield a quick knockdown in the right conditions. The key to success is having enough experience to know when to do it and when not to. Don and I have many years of experience fighting brush fires. We both figured it was the way to go.

The fire had gotten into some isolated pockets of thick grass and brush and was putting up five-foot flames. Before leaving the road, Don jumped out and started the pump, which is mounted on the back of the brush truck. The last thing you want to do is drive into a field that is on fire and not be able to start your pump! He told me to drive west down the paved road until we found a way into the adjacent stubble field and then double back to attack the firefront. Once we reached the burning edge of the left flank, I pointed the truck north so the reel on the right side of the truck faced the fire, no more than 50 feet from us. Don jumped out, pulled a bunch of hose off the reel, and headed for the flames. I got out, ran to the back of the truck, increased the pump pressure to 100 pounds per square inch (psi), and turned on the foam injector. My next job was to tend hose for Don until we were ready to advance. I pulled more hose off the reel and towards Don so he could more easily attack the flank. He then extinguished fire to the south far enough to tie in with the black Randy had created. This significantly decreased the odds the fire would wrap around us.

Don later told me he was surprised and frankly quite relieved he was able to knock the flames down as quickly as he did. Getting up close to five-foot flames in the middle of a grass field is intimidating enough. When the wind is blowing 20 mph, it can be downright scary. But now that the fire behind us was out, we knew we could safely chase the left flank as it headed north.

I jumped in the truck and slowly drove north and east, dodging large rocks and fence posts while Don put out the burning grass next to and ahead of us. Eventually, we were able to drive between two burned-out fence posts and drive over the fencing to get fully into the burnt part of the field. We were happy to be in the black.

Chief Jim Walkowski suddenly showed up on foot in his wildland gear. He gave us a big smile as he asked, "You guys want some help?" "Sure," I said. Jim grabbed the hose off the reel on the left side of the truck and headed north towards a large finger of fire that was progressing towards a structure. With Jim working up ahead and Don paralleling the truck, we quickly made progress to the north end of the field. We could see that E91 had arrived and moved in for structure protection to our left. That gave us confidence the house was safe.

I was beginning to scramble as I tried to support the two attack lines and advance the truck. Jim had moved forward and west about 100 feet, and from that far away, he could no longer pull the hose off the reel. When I saw this, I stopped the truck, jumped out and pulled off about 50 feet of hose for him, jumped back in the truck, and drove slowly forward about 50 to 100 feet. As I drove, I had to keep my eye on Don's progress and be sure not to drag him forward, run over his hose, or hit rocks and holes scattered throughout the field. Repeatedly, I jumped out and hauled in any extra hose accumulating on Jim's or Don's lines as the three of us converged. This continued for a hundred yards until we reached the heavy timber.

The fire had already gotten into the larger timber. Large and small Ponderosa Pine were torching with a loud whoosh and roar, but the fire progression was slowed because it was now backing down a steep hill and less exposed to the wind. Don and Jim went after the fire, weaving their ¾-inch hoselines between the trees until they ran out of hose 200 feet below the truck. They came back up the hill, and we extended a new 1 1/4 progressive hose 200 feet down the hill. Our hose packs would allow now us to extend the hoseline 600 feet, something you cannot do with the rubber hoses on the reels. We soon noticed that B92 had teamed up with B94 and were advancing down the hill with a progressive hoselay on the right flank. It was a welcomed site.

By this time, DNR had several brush trucks on the scene. They joined us as we worked through the heavy timber and brush, knocking down burning pockets of forest litter, downed timber, and torching trees. When all converged at the head of the fire, the forward progress of the fire was stopped. The initial attack, or IA as we call it, was a success. It had taken about an hour and a half to stop the fire. It would take several more hours to get it mopped up enough to turn it over to DNR and head home.

By 9:15 PM, we had made substantial progress getting the hot spots cooled down, and Chief Greg Anderson, the SCFD9 920 Officer, told us we could pack up and return to our station. We had been working on the fire for about three hours and were ready to head home. Although the sun was sinking fast, it was only visible as a burning reddish glow on the western horizon. Smoke from large fires in Washington, Oregon, and Canada filled the sky in every direction. It looked like a dark gray/brown soup that smelled of burned grass and timber. Working long hours in these smokey conditions always creates a tightness in your chest you try to ignore, but after working hard for several hours, the smoke and heat eventually get your attention. That tightness reminds you that breathing this air is very bad for your health, and the heat tells you this is a young person's game.

While collecting our hoses, we discovered we had burned a hole in one of our ¾-inch hoses. We also had 600 feet of 1 1/2-inch soot-covered wet progressive hose in a pile, so we just tossed it in the back of the truck. Usually, we reload all of our hoses in their specified locations before leaving a fire. But we decided we were close enough to our station that we would leave it tossed in the back of the truck. When we returned to the station, we planned to wash off all the soot, set the hoses out to dry, and reload clean, dry hoses from our inventory.

When we finally drove out of the field to Whipple Road, we found Lieutenant Gary had brought WT96 to the fire minutes after we arrived. He had helped fight the fire at the south end and used WT96 to provide water for the other brush trucks. Chief Anderson eventually asked Gary to get Jeep Plow 96 (P96) from Station 96 and use it to help the crews that were digging a hand trail around the fire. P96 is an old green 1974 4x4 Jeep with a single large farming disc (instead of an actual plow shear) welded on a hydraulic ram. The disc can be lowered off the back of the jeep to create multiple furrows in the dirt surrounding field fires like this one. It's a real worksaver. Luckily, we had another volunteer standing by at the station, and Gary had him drive the plow the short distance to the fire scene. Gary later told me he had a great time showing the new volunteer how to drive the jeep around the field. It's a challenging job but can be fun, and most of the guys at the station are eager to do it.

Gary was also getting ready to head back to the station in WT96. Don and I took some additional time to fill up B96 with water before heading to the station ourselves.

About a half mile from the station, Don radioed Dispatch to let them know we were released from the fire and were back in service (i.e., available to be dispatched if needed on another incident). Dispatch told us they had just received a report of a new fire at the intersection of North Forker Road and East Moffat Road. We were traveling north on Forker and had just passed the east end of Moffat but had seen nothing, and Don told them so. About two minutes later, at 9:45 PM, just as we were arriving at our station, they radioed back and said they had an additional report of the new fire on East Moffat Road about 1/4 mile west of Forker Road. At that instant, our pagers went off, dispatching us to this new fire. I immediately turned the truck around in a U-turn right in front of the station. Don hit the lights and sirens, and we were off to the fire. Gary stood on the station ramp, waiting to help us unload the truck. He looked a bit confused, perhaps wondering why we didn't tell him to join us on the truck. We felt bad leaving him, but we figured he might be needed to bring WT96 to this new fire, so it was best to leave him there.

We were on the scene of the new fire in about three minutes. It was a quarter of an acre on the north side of Moffat Road in brush and timber with flame lengths three to five feet high. There were also a few small trees torching. It had gotten very dark, so the flames and torching trees set against a dark forest background created an intimidating picture. We could see the lights of a house through the timber about 100 yards north of the fire and knew we needed to get the fire knocked down in a hurry. Don gave a size-up to Dispatch and asked for an additional brush truck and WT96. Gary was soon on his way to join us.

I parked on Moffat Road, blocking the westbound lane. Don grabbed the one remaining 3/4 inch hose off the real and headed up the steep eight-foot embankment to the fire. I started the pump, helped pull more hose off the reel, and dragged it up behind him. When I got up on the embankment, I saw the fire was heading north and west. Don was getting a good knockdown on the east side, but we needed a line around the left flank as well. I yelled to Don that I was going after the left flank and climbed down to the truck only to look at the tangle of hose stuffed in a pile in the back of the truck. I had one remaining option. We store one last hoseline on the truck that holds 200 feet of 1 3/4 hose called the "slot" load. It's heavier than our 1 1/2 progressive hose because it's double jacketed (two layers of hose rather than one), so it can be used on structure fires. I grabbed the slot load and deployed it on the road alongside the embankment. Because of its additional weight and the steepness of the embankment, there was no way I could carry it on my shoulder up the eight-foot embankment. Instead, I grabbed the nozzle and the first 12 feet of uncharged hose and started crawling up the embankment on my hands and knees. Once I got to the top, I pulled up another 20 feet hand over hand. When I stood up, I was surrounded by grass and brush that was on fire. I quickly slid on my ass down the embankment to the truck and opened the valve to fill the hose. Now that it was charged, I crawled back up the embankment, grabbed the nozzle, and started putting out fire as quickly as I could. Once I had extinguished everything I could reach, I hand-jacked more charged hose line up the embankment and then stretched the hose out to progress around the left flank. It sounds easy, but I was working at my maximum. Right about then, Chief Anderson pulled up in his pickup. Behind him was Gary in WT96. On my radio, I heard Greg tell Gary to keep going west on Moffat. There were two more fires a mile to the west, and he needed Gary to attack them along with B94, which had been reassigned from the Whipple fire to these two new fires.

"These guys (referring to me and Don) have this fire pretty much under control," Greg told Gary over the radio. I looked at Greg as Gary drove by, thinking this was no longer any fun.

Don and I both had deployed 200 feet of hose; he was on the right flank, and I was on the left. But we still couldn't reach the entire perimeter of the fire. With little or no enthusiasm, I struggled back down to the truck, put a 30-pound pack of progressive hose on my back, and scrambled back up the embankment on my hands and knees one more time. This time, I used the charged line as a climbing rope. Using 100 feet of hose from my pack, I extended the hose line and worked my way around the north flank, putting out the remaining fire. We had stopped the progression of the fire. We were both beat.

The two fires west of us were smaller, and B94 and Gary handled them quickly. Both fires were just below homes situated on the steep hill bordering the north side of Moffat Road. The quick work by Gary and B94 probably saved those homes.

A few hours later, we were finally back at the station, unloading and replacing all the filthy wet hoses. It was 1 AM before B96 was ready to go again. Don, Gary, and I soon headed home for a shower and a good night's sleep. Fortunately, there were no more fires that night.

All four of the fires that day had been intentionally set. Official investigations completed in the following weeks indicated they were all set by the same person. What goes on in people's minds when they set fires is a mystery to me and always will be. What goes on in the minds of people who volunteer to work long hours on the fireline in smoke and heat to put these fires out is simple: it needs to be done.

Chapter 9

On My Way!

In January of 2007, Steve Jobs unveiled the iPhone. It went on sale in June and cost $499. I first started seeing my colleagues at the university using the sleek black or white iPhones at meetings. They often set their iPhones on the table, occasionally using them to check their email or calendar. At the time, I was using a small flip phone with a tiny screen that made using the few clunky applications on the phone all but impossible. I could text with my phone, which was great, but every text cost ten cents.

I eventually bought my own iPhone in the fall of 2009. The deciding factor was that AT&T was giving our university employees a discount on both the iPhone and a phone plan. Best of all, you could get free unlimited texting and group texting. I knew texting would be an excellent tool for the volunteers at Station 96, and I was determined to get my fellow volunteers on board.

When I bought my iPhone, I created our first Station 96 text chain. I asked everyone who had unlimited texting to use the text chain to indicate if they were responding to the station each time we received a call on our pagers. This is when the phrase "On my way" became our way of communicating about who was coming and who wasn't. If a volunteer were unavailable, they would send "can't make it" or "No Dan" or something similar. Using group texting, we could quickly decide whether it was worth waiting for additional people to arrive or leave for the call as soon as we had a minimum of two people.

A second benefit of the text chain was identifying who was going straight to the scene POV. When a call was close to someone's home, they could text "POV," indicating they were taking their personally owned vehicle (abbreviated POV) directly to the scene. Such POV responses have proven critical for EMS calls. For example, in one instance, Jon responded to a neighbor's home on a call for a young boy who had attempted suicide. Jon was the first EMS person on the scene and helped one of the parents save the boy's life.

Other benefits of using our text chain included communicating who would be available for responses when severe weather conditions were imminent, such as Red Flag Warnings or severe storms. We also began using the text chain to communicate and plan for responses to fires occurring in neighboring districts. Over time, our text chain communications have become central to everything we do. So much so that when I told the station volunteers I would title my book "On My Way!" they thought it was perfect.

The evolution of the smartphone also helped create some of our most recent advances in district-wide emergency communications. When Dispatch sends out a call, it now arrives on our smartphones as two texts. The first text contains the same information that comes to our physical pagers: the type of incident, radio channel, all assigned units, the map book page, the nearest cross street, and an incident number. The second text contains a Google Map image with a pin dropped on the incident's location. The map page lets us get GPS coordinates, map the quickest route, visually identify how many units can access the scene, and tentatively identify landing zones for a helicopter.

Other new digital tools are also making us more efficient. For example, each engine and brush truck now carries a mobile data terminal (MDT) (i.e., a smartphone or computer tablet dedicated to our truck) that has Internet and cellular data access and a built-in automatic vehicle location system (AVL). The AVL has a built-in GPS linked to Dispatch's computer-aided dispatch systems (CADS). Consequently, the location of every District 9 engine, brush truck, and career officer's response vehicle is simultaneously tracked by GPS and integrated into dispatching assignments. All this information is displayed in real-time on satellite maps on our trucks' dedicated devices. Adopting this technology ensures the closest available resource is dispatched to every incident and enables responding units to track all incoming responding units.

The most critical positive outcome of using all the new digital technology is a decrease in our response times to an incident. This one outcome is crucial because fire science literature is unequivocal that decreased response times are positively correlated with improved outcomes for both fire and EMS emergencies.

Chapter 10

Did He Say Eleven-Oh-Six?

Whenever we arrive on the scene of an accident, medical emergency, or fire and discover a deceased victim, we communicate this information to Dispatch by telling them we have a confirmed 11-06 (pronounced "eleven-oh-six"). Try as I might, I have not been able to track down the origin of the 11-06 code. There are numerous standard 10-codes and 11-codes used by law enforcement, fire, and EMS nationwide. But the term 11-06 is not one of them. A local official from the Spokane County Dispatch Service recently told me that he believed the 11-06 code was created many years ago by the Spokane County Medical Examiner. It was intended for use by all fire and EMS in Spokane County.

On Sunday, July 24, 2016, I rode my XLK250 through the woods to the station, responding to a 46D, an MVA with life-threatening injuries. I was the third volunteer to arrive at the station. Captain Don was already sitting in the officer's seat in E96. Matt, who lives across the street from the station, was in the driver's seat. I scrambled into my turnouts as quickly as possible, trotted out to the running truck, and climbed in. We immediately rolled out of the bay with lights and sirens and headed south on Forker Road. The accident was a head-on involving two vehicles on Bigelow Gulch Road. The accident scene was about two miles south of the station.

In 2016, Bigelow Gulch was a narrow two-lane county road running east-west with numerous large dips and tall sharp crests. The speed limit was 45, but most people drove 60 mph. It was a straight road, but the dips and crests blocked your view of what was coming over the next crest. The surface was a combination of cracked asphalt, raised asphalt patches, and scattered potholes. It was a dangerous road. The only thing that separated cars traveling 50 to 60 mph in opposite directions was a faded double yellow line.

When E94 arrived on the scene, they called for a second ambulance and upgraded the call to an extrication call. This upgrade added Rescue 92 (R92) and the District 920 Officer. When we arrived on the scene no more than five minutes after responding, we were told by 920 to park at the east end of the incident, block the road with E96, and walk up to the scene to help with extrication and patient care.

The accident was at the peak of a large crest in the road. It was a hot walk up the 15% grade in our boots and turnouts. The asphalt had been baking all day in the July sun, and we could see the heat reflecting off the road as we approached. Although it was after 8 PM, it was 80 degrees and dead calm.

Both cars were compacts, one a Honda, the other a Chevy. The front ends of both cars were heavily damaged. The two were separated by about 40 feet, and it was evident from the damage and their positions in the road that the force of impact was significant enough to cause them to bounce off of one another. As we walked through the scene, I felt an uncomfortable familiarity with all the sounds and smells of a severe accident. Multiple fire truck diesel engines chugged along at idle, distant sirens howled from incoming resources, and a mix of radio and verbal communications could be heard throughout the scene. On a scene like this, it's always all business. There are no greetings, no chit-chat, and no smiles. The environment is saturated with the business of getting things done.

Our first task was to help extract a male patient from the east-bound Honda. Don and I used a backboard to help remove a large male, about 30 years old, from the front passenger seat. He was in a lot of pain and screamed when we slid him out onto the board. An ambulance crew took him straight into one of the waiting ambulances.

An uninjured child was found in a car seat in the back of the car. The child was now in the arms of a firefighter who was told to hold and comfort the child until a better option became available. The driver of the Honda was the injured man's wife. She had gotten out of the car on her own and was nowhere to be seen.

Matt was sent to the Chevy to assist as the crew from E94 used the jaws of life to pry open the driver's door, bending it out of the way. Once the elderly male driver was extracted, again using a backboard, the medics took over and moved him to an ambulance. He had a rigid abdomen, indicating significant internal injuries. He was a load-and-go and the ambulance wasted no time heading to the hospital.

In the passenger seat was an elderly woman. She was still strapped in her seat belt. Her head and torso were slumped forward. She was an 11-06. Matt was told to open the passenger side door with the jaws and reposition the victim so she wouldn't slide out of the car. It's standard for us to leave deceased victims where we find them, if possible. When law enforcement takes over the scene, they collect whatever information they need for their investigation, and only then do we extricate the victims. This was the first deceased victim Matt had ever worked on, and to this day, it bothers him to talk about it. It never gets easy.

Our next assignment was to provide patient care for the driver of the Honda. She was a woman in her 30s, and we found her sitting on the tailboard of E94. She was complaining of severe shoulder pain. I quickly went through the usual sequence of assessing her to determine the extent of her injuries. She had elevated heart and respiratory rates, dilated pupils, and slightly elevated systolic blood pressure. She was alert and showed no signs of head, neck, or back injuries. Her only physical injury was to her shoulder. She was in a lot of pain and holding her arm across her chest, which suggested either a shoulder dislocation or a broken clavicle. Fortunately, she had been wearing a seat belt, which, together with the airbag, probably saved her life.

During my assessment, she became increasingly agitated. The shock of the accident was gradually wearing off, and she started to have an anxiety attack. She became unable to tolerate any movement of her arm and was increasingly animated. As we attempted to sling and swath her shoulder, she began rapidly asking questions about the accident, her husband, the baby, and the people in the other vehicle. I told her the other crews were doing everything they could and asked her to focus on staying calm. In a moment of relative silence, we all heard the incident commander inform Dispatch we had multiple patients being transported, and one confirmed 11-06.

"Did he say eleven-oh-six?" our patient asked. "I know what that means! That means someone died! Oh my god, did I kill somebody?"

I said nothing. At the time, I had no idea how the accident happened, and my immediate reaction was a mix of empathy and suspicion. What could have happened, I wondered? What could she have done for her to ask if she had killed somebody? As I tried to put it out of my mind, Chris, a District 9 medic, stepped up and asked for a patient update. I gave him the update, and he took over patient care. Chris thanked me and suggested we find Incident Command and get another reassignment. As we walked away, I could hear the patient pressing Chris for answers. I was glad to move on to something else, anything else.

Our next assignment was to help clean up the scene. We put away all the extrication gear and waited for the tow trucks. During the final minutes of cleaning up, various crew members discussed the events leading up to the crash. The gist was that the younger couple in the eastbound car were having an argument that became physical to the point that the wife was hitting and biting her husband while she was driving. The husband demanded she pull over and let him out, but she refused. Somehow, just as their car crested a crest in the road, it drifted over the center line and hit the westbound car head-on. The elderly couple in the westbound car probably never saw it coming. The woman was killed instantly. Her husband was critically injured but survived.

As the years have passed, I've always wondered how our patient knew what 11-06 meant. As I explained at the beginning of this story, it's a code only used by fire and EMS in Spokane County. Perhaps, at one time, she, her husband, a family member, or a friend was a first responder. I'll never know. I don't want to know.

I recently found an old Internet article about the accident. The driver of the eastbound car was arrested soon after arriving at the hospital and booked for vehicular homicide and vehicular assault. She was alleged to be driving with a suspended license. I don't know if she was ultimately convicted of any crimes. What I do know is that I hope no one I'm treating at an MVA ever asks me that question again.

Bigelow Gulch Road has recently been widened and flattened, and a median has been added in some places. Unfortunately, the improvements were seven years too late for the elderly couple in that westbound car. The improvements won't fix the tragic loss. And they won't erase the images of the victims from the minds of the first responders. This might be the hardest part of being a first responder. You sometimes see people suffer when there is little or nothing you can do. You see them in your mind over and over for the rest of your life. Somehow, you have to balance that fact with those moments when you feel good about the work you do.

Chapter 11

Welfare Check

Occasionally, we get a call for a welfare check. The call is always assigned as a 31A (the alpha code indicating minor or unknown injuries). The issue could be a variety of things, but a 31A indicates that someone is, or might be, in need of assistance. The situation often begins when an individual calls 911 because they are concerned about someone. It then becomes the responsibility of the local fire department to determine if the person of concern is all right. Sometimes, the caller hasn't recently seen or been able to contact the person. The caller could be a next-door neighbor or a family member living in another state thousands of miles away. Sometimes, the caller is just a passerby who sees a person behaving oddly in a public place and believes that person needs our help. Often, but not always, the person of concern is elderly or disabled in some way. In all these scenarios, the caller takes on the initial role of the Good Samaritan. The role then is passed to the fire department. This is a story about such a call.

On a Tuesday night in June of 2022, the Station 96 crew was beginning our usual Tuesday-night training when I got a phone call from Peggy, a friend of mine who lives up on Forker Ridge. Forker Ridge is accessed by Judkins Lane, a private lane that serves about 25 homes. I know the area well because from 1996 to 2008, I lived just off of Judkins Lane on Black Bear Lane. Peggy called me to tell me she had just received a call from a local friend concerned about one of their neighbors. He had not seen the neighbor in about two weeks. He said this was unusual, and he was concerned about her welfare. The neighbor was a woman in her late fifties. She lived alone in a house on a ten-acre parcel of land and was active in the community. She was well known for sheltering numerous animals on her property, such as geese, ducks, and rabbits. I told Peggy we'd be happy to do a welfare check if she would call 911 and make the request so we would get a page from Dispatch. This would also trigger a call for E94, with a Paramedic on board. Peggy agreed. A few minutes later, Peggy called back to let me know that 911 had been called.

I explained to the crew what was happening, and four of us, Don, myself, Gavin, and Mark, climbed into B96 and headed up to Judkins Lane.

When the official page from Dispatch came a minute later, I knew the address well. When I lived in the Judkins Lane area, I knew the couple that had built the house and shop that still sit on the property. Since 2008, the property has changed hands several times. We had a medical call there about three years ago. Matt was the only responder from Station 96. Here are the details of that call.

It was January 31, 2020, at 2:50 AM. Matt went solo in B96 to assist the crew on E94. Forker Ridge gets a lot of snow in the winter, and Matt knew that taking B96, with four-wheel drive, was the smart thing to do. Matt ended up driving the officer and medic from E94 in B96 the last 1 1/2 miles of tight, winding, snow-covered road to the property. The call was for a middle-aged woman suffering from disorientation and difficulty breathing. The front door was locked when they arrived on the scene, and they could hear the woman calling for help from inside the house. They quickly found a window by the house's front deck that was not locked and climbed through it.

They found the patient lying naked on the floor in the hallway between her bedroom and the bathroom. She had fallen and couldn't get up. The house reeked of animal feces, stale food, and stale air. Chickens, rabbits, and ducks wandered throughout the house. The floor was covered with straw, animal scat, discarded boxes, and other refuse. Matt said that the smell of feces and urine was nauseating.

Firefighters are trained to work in all sorts of stressful environments, and this was no different. The crew assessed the patient, determined she needed to go to the hospital, and loaded her into the waiting ambulance. An hour later, everyone was back in bed.

Because I knew Judkins Lane exceptionally well, we made the long, twisty drive relatively quickly. The homeowner's old, faded green Subaru was parked in front of the house with grass and weeds growing up around the wheels. It was full of stuff and looked like it hadn't been driven for a while. The yard contained several outbuildings and small fenced areas but no animals. We tried knocking on the front door with no response, then did our usual three-sixty of the home (meaning we walked entirely around it), peeking in through all the windows and trying all the doors. The house was locked and dark. We also did a three-sixty of the large metal shop and a single-wide trailer. We could see a large white rabbit moving around in one of the house's bedrooms. Several geese and ducks were wandering around in the shop.

When E94 arrived, Captain Don gave their Captain, Dan Garner, an update. Dan ran the siren on E94 to see if that would get anyone from the house to answer the front door, but no one showed. In the meantime, Mark found a window on the south side of the house that wasn't locked. He opened the window, and an awful smell tumbled out. I told Mark, "I think there's a dead body in there." "Sure smells like it," he said.

After some discussion, Captain Dan and Captain Don volunteered to climb through the window and search the house. After sticking cotton up their nostrils and donning N95 masks, gloves, and glasses, they climbed through the window. They soon returned to confirm the homeowner was deceased. She was lying in her bed under a blanket. It was evident she had been there for a week or more. There were also chickens and several rabbits in the house. The home's condition was just as Matt had found it a year and a half ago.

Don updated Dispatch and asked for a response from the Sheriff's office, which is standard procedure. The rest of the crew broke open all the locked outbuildings, suspecting they contained other animals. Geese and ducks scrambled out from three of the four buildings. We filled three kiddy pools we found in the yard with water from a frost-free hydrant so all the animals could have a drink. The animals immediately scurried to the pools to drink.

Because it was 10 PM, animal control was unavailable that night. Their response would be delayed until tomorrow. We decided to leave the animals to roam freely about the yard.

The Sheriff eventually arrived, and Captain Dan filled him in. The Sheriff said he'd wait to enter the house until the next-in patrol officer arrived. He told us he wanted to wait because the next-in officer was a "new guy," and this would be his first DOA (dead on arrival). He figured the new guy would benefit from the experience.

I called my friend Peggy on my cell phone and gave her the unfortunate news. We talked a bit about the animals, and both felt leaving it up to animal control was the best solution. Peggy said she'd call the neighbor who had called her and let him know what we found.

During all this, I decided it was best to go into the house and look around. I didn't want to, but I thought I might learn something. I donned an N95 mask, gloves, and glasses and walked through the house. It was just as the guys described. The one thing I learned was that there are sights and smells you can't un-see or un-smell. I found a large bowl, filled it with fresh water, and left it for the two large rabbits that refused to leave the house.

Later that night, I asked myself: what drives someone to arrive at a place like this? How can it be explained to family and loved ones? Is it madness or just an unexpected but inevitable small probability of "normal" behavior? In the end, the most positive thing I can say is that even for someone like this unfortunate woman, others cared enough to be concerned for her and acted on her behalf by trying to help.

Chapter 12

Who's Gonna Take The Dog?

Most of our neighbors have dogs, and it's not unusual to see them walking their dogs along the roadside. This story is about a woman and her husband, who, for many years, walked their dogs along East Moffat Road.

Moffat Road is a moderately busy paved county road. It carries traffic between Peone Prairie and the Foothills. Before it was paved 15 years ago, it was a seldom-traveled dusty gravel road used mainly by the locals. Going back to the early 1900s, Moffat was little more than a dirt trail used by horse-drawn US mail wagons to deliver mail between the Mead Post Office and the Foothills area. Before that, local lore indicates it was a game trail used in the 1800s by the Spokane Indian tribe. I imagine many county roads in Spokane have origin stories that deserve telling. But I digress. My main point is that any road, old or new, becomes a part of the lives of the people who travel it.

When I moved to the Foothills area in 1996, Moffat Road was gravel. One of the things I remember most about traveling along Moffat is that I regularly saw a woman and a man walking their dog along the narrow edge of the road. The couple were middle-aged, both tall and thin. I'm unsure if it was always the same dog, but it was always mid-sized and walked dutifully along on a leash.

Because it's considered rude not to, whenever I came upon them, I always slowed considerably and tried to keep the billowing dust cloud behind my vehicle to a minimum as I passed. The woman always gave a small wave of thanks, which I returned. She didn't often look at me when she waved. Usually, she only tossed a subtle wave in my direction while walking along, constantly looking down at the road as if afraid to make a misstep. The man never waved or even acknowledged my passing. He looked right past me in a way that made me think that perhaps I should apologize for my presence on the road. I never did apologize. But I always wondered why on earth they walked their dogs on the edge of such a dry and dusty gravel road that had no shoulder.

Eventually, Moffat Road was paved with chip-seal in the early 2000s and soon became much busier. Nowadays, instead of the occasional car or farm truck crawling along on the slippery and noisy gravel at 15 or 20 mph, people fly along the pavement at 50 or 60 mph in their shiny pickups, sports cars, and SUVs. Yet, despite the increased high-speed traffic, I still regularly would come across my tall and thin neighbors walking their dog along the narrow edge of the road. A few years back, the frequency of my sightings of them began to decrease. I'm not sure exactly when, but eventually, I would only see the woman walking the dog.

On July 20, 2017, we had a 31B, or bravo call, indicating a non-life-threatening medical situation. The 31B was for difficulty breathing with an address on East Moffat Road. As usual, I responded by riding through the woods on my KXL250, finding Captain Don waiting for me in B96. Once on the road, we were confident we would beat E94 to the house because 31B calls are no-code responses. Consequently, E94 would be responding without lights and sirens. Captain Don and I arrived at the house and drove around back. As we climbed the wooden steps of the back porch, we noticed a dozen or more green D-sized oxygen bottles staged by the door. Some were still in opened cardboard boxes wearing their customary white plastic seal. Others had no seal, indicating they had been used and were probably empty. Before we reached the door, it opened, and I was a bit surprised to recognize the tall, thin woman holding the door as the woman I had seen for years walking her dog on Moffat Road.

The woman's name was Madeline. She slowly led us through the kitchen into the living room to John, her husband. John was sitting in an old, worn leather recliner, wearing an oxygen mask and having difficulty breathing. There were several of the green oxygen bottles staged next to his chair. We soon learned John suffered from late-stage Chronic Obstructive Pulmonary Disease (COPD). I performed a quick assessment that revealed a low oxygen saturation despite the supplemental oxygen> he also had an elevated heart rate and blood pressure. He was also irritable, which was not surprising given his condition. Soon after E94 and the ambulance arrived, John was loaded into the ambulance and on his way to the hospital.

As Don and I exited the kitchen door and walked onto the porch, we now fully understood the collection of oxygen bottles sitting by the back door. What especially caught my attention was something I had missed earlier.

Next to the cache of oxygen bottles was an old, weathered kitchen chair and an ashtray filled with light gray ash and cigarette butts. As we loaded our gear, I couldn't help but think I'd likely never again see John walking along the roadside with his wife and dog. In my experience, people with COPD who continue to smoke don't live very long.

There were fewer sightings of Madeline walking her dog after the day we sent John to the hospital. When I did see her, she was usually close to home, walking very slowly on the lower, less steep part of Moffat Road.

On July 7, 2021, we received a 31D medical call for difficulty breathing at Madeline's and John's address. To my surprise, our patient was Madeline, not John. Engine 92 had beaten us to the house, and their medic was assessing Madeline in the living room when we walked in. Based on her level of discomfort and vitals, the medic strongly recommended she go to the hospital. Reluctantly, she agreed to go. John was in the living room, sitting in his leather chair with a nose cannula on his face and breathing slowly from one of his oxygen bottles. The dog was lying in the corner of the room, watching Madeline. As we walked out onto the back porch, I remember once again seeing the large cache of oxygen bottles, the kitchen chair, and a well-used ashtray.

I don't believe I ever saw Madeline or John again until two weeks ago, on October 12, 2022. It was an unusually warm and sunny October morning when we were again paged for a 31D at their home.

I arrived at the station finding Captain Don sitting in B96. We were quickly on the road with lights and sirens. Don asked Dispatch for the short. They replied, "You have an 82-year-old male with hand and facial burns received while changing his oxygen bottle. Engine 92 and AMR 109 are responding, and Life Flight has been launched."

Our 930 Officer (the District's Safety Officer, Captain Rob Bault) soon came over the radio, added himself to the call, and told Dispatch he would be "ground contact" for the helo. As we weaved our way west down through the S-curves of Moffat Road, Don and I anticipated we'd get on the scene at about the same time as E92, approaching from the west.

When we arrived, we parked on Moffat with E92, leaving the driveway to the back porch clear for the ambulance. The medic from E92 and I walked up the short circular gravel driveway towards the back entry of the house. On our way up the driveway, we ran into a neighbor who was coming down from the house. I asked if the patient was conscious and alert.

He replied, "Yeah, John's conscious, but he's kind of ornery."

"Is Madeline with him?"

"No, she passed in December."

I nodded and headed to the porch. I was surprised by the news of Madeline's passing. I never expected her to go first.

The medic was just ahead of me as we climbed the steps to the porch. There on the porch by the door was a small pile of ash and what looked like a melted face mask. The back door to the kitchen was open. John was sitting on a stool in the middle of the kitchen. He was holding his burned hands out in front of him on his lap. His shirt was open to the waist, and his face, eyebrows, and hair were burned. The medic asked me to get some vitals while he spoke to John.

I pulled the pulse oximeter from E92's Life-Pack 1500 and gently placed it on his right index finger, which appeared not to be burned. John immediately pulled it off and started to fidget with it with the fingers of his left hand. I was about to put the pulse oximeter back on his finger when the medic said, "We need to get his shirt off. Let's get an ECG."

I thought about cutting his shirt off, but John was in a bad mood, and most conscious patients don't like us cutting off their clothes. His flannel shirt was already unbuttoned and hanging loosely on his thin frame, so I took it off one arm at a time. He wasn't happy with me and complained gruffly about his hands being burned, but off it came.

John's mood was deteriorating, and the medic decided it was best to give up trying to get vitals or an ECG and get him on a gurney and into the arriving ambulance. John would need an induction agent (a non-barbiturate-sedative, which depresses central nervous system function) and rapid intubation before his helicopter ride to the hospital. That could be accomplished more quickly in the ambulance, and everything else could wait.

After putting John in the ambulance, I started to walk down the driveway. John's dog had been somewhere in the house and now had come out to the driveway. He was wandering around, as if he was trying to understand what was going on. One of the crew from E94 asked, "Who's gonna take the dog?"

"I'll take him; I live next door; it's not a problem," said the neighbor I had spoken with earlier. Problem solved.

Gary had arrived on the scene POV, so he and I grabbed safety vests and stop signs from B96 and took up positions east and west of the scene to stop any traffic on Moffat Road. As the helo arrived overhead, Rob, our 930 Officer, stood in the middle of a grass field across the road from the house, slowly waving a long stick with an even longer piece of orange plastic tape attached to the end. He was talking to the helo on the radio. They quickly circled the field and then dropped in from the west, landing softly.

The ambulance had just driven down the driveway and parked on Moffat. A medical crew of two exited the helo and walked across the field with their gear. They had a brief discussion with the medic from E94 and climbed into the back of the ambulance. Five minutes later, the helo crew and the gurney exited the ambulance. John was lying on the gurney, unconscious, intubated, and had been given an IV. Don and the crew from E94 quickly moved the gurney across the field to the running helo. John was loaded onto the bird, and off they went, making a beeline for the nearest hospital.

At around noon the next day, I received a text from Captain Don letting me know that John had died. He had suffered severe burns to his airway, and nothing could be done.

We don't always know the outcome of our efforts to help patients. When we do know, news that a patient didn't make it is always a punch in the gut. Just yesterday, I was talking to John, trying to get his shirt off without hurting him. Now he's gone. Both he and Madeline, my tall and thin neighbors who I'd seen walking their dog along Moffat Road for over two decades, were gone.

I'm sure there will be many times I'll think of Madeline and John when I drive by their former home on Moffat Road. And maybe, just maybe, I'll see their neighbor walking their dog. That would be nice.

Chapter 13

Where's My Girlfriend?

We had a call for an MVA about 20 years ago on East Moffat Road. It was a motorcycle accident. The accident scene was on the east 1200 block of Moffat near my house, so I responded POV. The 1200 block contains a series of S-curves that drop down the draw as you drive westward. On the north border of the road is a steep ridge with just enough room for a few well-placed homes that hide in the timber. To the south is a series of long, narrow wheat and grass fields that drop steeply down to the bottom of the draw containing Peone Creek. It's a steep ten-foot drop-off from the road into the fields at the upper end of the S-curves. This is precisely where the accident occurred.

I arrived in the area and found an SUV with its emergency flashers on. It was parked on the very edge of the eastbound lane with a man standing behind it. Another man was sitting on the side of the road facing the field below. A motorcycle helmet sat on the ground next to him.

I drove past the SUV and parked, put my flashers on, and walked over to the man standing in the road. I was wearing a District 9 tee shirt and hat and was donning EMS gloves as I approached him. He immediately said he was the one who called 911. He had come upon the young man sitting by the side of the road, so he pulled over and asked him if he was OK. The man with the helmet said he had crashed his motorcycle and complained of a terrible headache. I thanked the caller and walked over to assess the man sitting on the road's edge. I could see pieces of black and white plastic scattered on the road's edge, along with a few scrapes and gouges in the chip-sealed surface of the road. The scrapes ran straight off the road's edge just past the apex of a right-hand curve. When I reached the rider, I took a position below him on the embankment so I could speak to him face-to-face.

"Hi, I'm with the Fire Department. I understand you fell off your motorcycle."

"Yeah," he said softly.

I picked up and examined his helmet for damage. Based on the condition of his helmet, I knew he had taken a pretty good hit to the head. I also knew from years of riding and racing motorcycles back in the 1980s that when someone crashes and then just sits there, showing no interest in what's happening around them, they've had their bell rung. I was worried.

I looked him in the eyes and asked, "What's your name?"

"Jorge."

"Do you have any injuries, Jorge?"

"No. I just have a bad headache."

"Jorge, is it OK if I examine you to see if you have other injuries?"

"OK," he said, looking past me into the grass field.

I quickly palpated his neck, spine, shoulders, arms and hands, legs and ankles. All negative for apparent injuries. Jorge was now looking down at the ground in front of him.

"Where's my girlfriend?" he asked softly as he turned his gaze up to me.

"Why? Was your girlfriend with you?"

"Yeah."

"Your girlfriend was on the back of your bike when you crashed?"

He nodded up and down, blankly staring at me.

Oh Fuck! I thought.

I turned around and looked out at the field behind me. All I saw was ten acres of curing four-foot-tall grass. The field sloped steeply away from the road, and there was nothing in the field but tall grass: no motorcycle, no girlfriend.

Just then, Jon, one of our volunteers, who also came POV, walked up to us. I turned to Jon.

"Jon, this is Jorge. It looks like he was headed west and went off the road right here. He was wearing a helmet but took a pretty good hit. He's got a bad headache, probably a concussion. No other injuries I know of. The problem is, he says his girlfriend was riding on the back. We need to see if she's down in the field somewhere."

"Got it. Find the girlfriend," Jon replied and headed down into the field.

I could see and hear E92 climbing up the road from the west, lights, and sirens. As soon as they parked, the medic climbed out and walked over to me and Jorge. I gave him the same update I had given Jon and turned patient care over to him. Then, I walked over to the officer of E92, who was walking towards us.

"We believe there was a passenger on the motorcycle, and she is somewhere in that field," I said.

Just then, E96 came around the corner from the east and parked.

"Take the crew off 96 and start griding the field," he said.

"Got it."

I walked over to Don and Gary as they climbed out of the engine and quickly explained the situation. We all headed down into the field and joined Jon. He described the area he had already covered and told us he had found the motorcycle but not the girlfriend.

We quickly planned to systematically search a larger area from where Jorge had left the road to about 40 yards past the crumpled bike. We formed a line perpendicular to the road, standing an arm's length apart, and walked parallel to the road from east to west, then returned west to east just below our initial pass. We repeated the process until we had covered the area from the road to about 40 yards below the crashed motorcycle. We found nothing but scattered bits of the bike.

While we were searching the field, the crew on E92 were able to contact Jorge's parents by phone. They lived a few miles away on North Forker Road. The parents were able to contact Jorge's girlfriend by phone, which verified she was not, in fact, with Jorge when he crashed. Obviously, Jorge's crash left him more than a bit confused.

Once Jorge was transported to the hospital, we cleaned up the accident scene and returned to the station. It had been a rather unique call, to say the least. The primary emotion of the day was relief that Jorge was by himself. We all had disturbing pictures in our minds of what we might have found in that field.

No matter how many years have passed, I am often reminded of Jorge's accident. I travel Moffat Road regularly, and whenever I drive around the sharp blind curve that Jorge failed to negotiate, I often think of him. Jorge was lucky he was alone, and even luckier, no one was coming up the road in the other direction.

Several years after his accident, we started getting regular EMS calls sending us to a North Forker address for a male patient who has seizures whenever he fails to take his medication. The first time we went on one of these calls, the short we received from Dispatch included the order to "Stand back for law." This short means we must not enter the residence until law enforcement ensures the scene is safe. It makes us all significantly more apprehensive about what we might find on scene.

Dispatch had called for law enforcement because the patient, recovering from his seizure, became physically aggressive with his parents, who live with him. It was standard procedure for law enforcement to be called to ensure everyone's safety.

When we receive stand back for law instructions, we respond to the neighborhood of the address and then slow our approach, turning off our lights and sirens. When we arrive in the area, we park out of sight of the residence until law enforcement tells Dispatch the scene is safe enough for us to enter and treat the patient.

On our first time responding to one of these calls on North Forker, we were soon cleared to enter the home and discovered that the patient was Jorge. We didn't recognize him immediately, but his father told us that his seizures resulted from a head injury from a motorcycle injury on Moffat Road a few years ago. We put the pieces together immediately.

Over the past ten years, we've been to Jorge's home over a dozen times. On each occasion, Jorge has been off his medication, resulting in a series of grand mal seizures. During his slow recovery from the seizure, Jorge is sullen, confused, angry, and sometimes physically threatening to his parents. He often takes off his clothes and wanders around outside naked. We know he understands and speaks English, but after a seizure, he speaks only in Spanish and usually screams at us and his parents using what my colleagues who speak Spanish tell me are rather creative curse words.

Since that initial call to his home, it has gotten a little easier to help Jorge. Over the years, we have learned that his confusion and anger gradually pass. All we have to do is wait long enough and give him the space he needs. Eventually, he becomes receptive to our help. If you rush him, his behavior deteriorates. His parents have also learned to give him the space and time he needs, but it can still be very stressful for everyone.

I decided to write about this story because what happened to Jorge has caused me to wonder more and more about what a patient's future might be after we put them in the ambulance. Will they recover? Will we see them again? We never really know. We can only hope for the best. When I think about it, being a volunteer *requires* hope, sometimes, a lot of it. They don't teach you that in the Firefighter Academy or EMS class. You learn it on the job.

Chapter 14

The Peone North Fire

On August 12, 2014, a haboob came through Spokane. If you are unfamiliar with haboobs, take a moment to search for images of haboobs online. They are impressive and frightening, especially during wildland fire season.

Haboob winds can often hit 60 mph, creating a billowing wall of dust that can rise to 10,000 feet in altitude and drop visibility to zero. People usually think haboobs happen only in the desert. However, residents of Eastern Washington know haboobs well. This is because the late summer harvesting of 1.8 million acres of farmland in Eastern Washington exposes the topsoil to winds driven by weather fronts moving in from the coast.

August 12 was a Tuesday night, our training night at Station 96. We usually meet at the station at 6:00 PM, perform maintenance checks on our trucks and equipment, and then train until 9:00 PM. Because of a forecasted haboob, Captain Don and I decided to go to the station early to prepare for the haboob. We've done this sort of thing many times over the years. Sometimes, we don't get an emergency call. But that doesn't concern us because we enjoy sitting in the station, drinking coffee, and listening to radio traffic from other stations responding to their calls. On this occasion, the call for us came, and we were ready.

The temperature that day peaked at 90 degrees around 3:00 PM. It was overcast and humid. A warm wind was blowing at six mph out of the northeast. Three hours later, at 6:00 PM, it was 87 degrees, but the wind had stiffened to 12 mph. Thirty-five minutes later, at 6:35 PM, the temperature had dropped to 72 degrees. The wind jumped to 47 mph and swung around to the southwest. These high winds brought tons of blowing dust and dropped the visibility to less than a quarter of a mile. The haboob had arrived.

I remember standing with Don outside the station dressed in our wildland gear. We were looking west, watching the storm roll in. The radio calls of other stations for downed power lines and brush fires hopscotched through Spokane County. They started in District 3, which covers the county's southwest corner. They next popped up in District 10 and the city of Spokane. Finally, calls started happening in the southwest portion of SCFD9. We knew the Foothills would be next. As we stood outside the station, the wind whipped up dust, leaves, and small branches in every direction. We joked nervously that we probably wouldn't get a call.

By 6:45 PM, Gary, Gabe, Jon, and Theo had arrived at the station. We were starting to smell the smoke of burning grass and brush, but all we could see on the horizon was thick brown/gray blowing dust. It was frustrating and nerve-racking to know that wind-blown fires were starting to eat up acres of land while we had to sit and wait for our pagers to go off. We knew from experience that driving around in the blowing dust looking for fire was a rookie mistake, and it's been a long time since Don and I were rookies. But we still wanted to get to work.

At 6:50 PM, our pagers started beeping. The call was for a 14H about 5 miles northwest of Station 96 at the north end of Peone Road. Don, Gabe, and I piled into B96 and headed off lights and sirens. Jon grabbed WT96 while Gary and Theo responded in E96.

As we headed north on Peck Road, Dispatch gave a short to all incoming units, telling us we had a one-acre wheat field fire with several structures threatened. We could see the glow from the fire once we dropped down off of North Heglar Road to Highway 206. Getting closer, we could see several 60-foot Ponderosa Pine trees standing in the backyard of a large residence lighting off like giant torches. The flames reached high above the heavy, dark gray smoke that was being blown sideways, staying low to the ground. The blowing dust and smoke made it impossible to see what was burning southwest of the trees.

Our District Chief, Jack Cates, arrived on the scene and took command of the fire. He had diverted from a nearby fire and was the first resource on the scene. Approaching the fire, we could see at least three acres of wind-driven fire moving fast in grass and wheat. Three old cedar-sided barns were already on fire; two were fully involved, and the third was just starting to burn as the grass fire rapidly surrounded it. Just to the southwest was a very old two-story farmhouse that didn't appear to be on fire.

Chief Cates had parked his command SUV in the driveway of a large, newly built home 50 yards north of the fire. The tall pines behind the house were still torching, but the firefront that set them ablaze had moved past the back of the house and was heading for a wheat field. Cates saw us pull up and told us to back in the driveway and provide structural protection for the residence.

I quickly backed into the driveway and parked just off the southwest corner of the house, with Don acting as my spotter. Gabe jumped out, and he and Don started pulling the 3/4-inch line off the passenger-side hose reel. They both headed towards the grass fire as it approached us. I hustled to the back of the truck, started the pump, turned on the foam, and set the pressure to 120 psi.

Don advanced the nozzle towards the fire while Gabe dragged more hose off the reel. I ran over to Gabe, grabbed the hose, and yelled over the roar of the wind and fire, "Gabe, get your helmet and gloves on. Now!"

Gabe stopped in his tracks, saying, "Oh shit!" He ran for the truck.

Gabe was relatively new at Station 96 and was so pumped with adrenaline that he hadn't noticed he wasn't wearing his PPE. A moth to the flame.

By now, the fire was climbing up the sides of the third cedar barn. The barn was about 30 feet wide by 50 feet long and two stories high. The dry cedar siding was crackling and popping, burning hot and fast. It began throwing massive amounts of radiant heat and embers at us and the house we were trying to protect.

As I pulled more hose from the real, I saw Don trying to hit the approaching grass fire. The wind was pushing against the spray from the nozzle turning it 90-degrees away from the fire. It evaporated in midair. I'd never seen that before, and it suddenly struck me that our direct attack was pointless.

As I approached Don, he turned to me, smiled, and yelled, "I guess we'll have to wait for the fire to come to us!" "Copy that," I yelled back. The wind and raging fire had gotten so loud I read his lips more than I heard him.

The heat from the burning barn was overwhelming. Heat travels in several forms, and we were hit with a double whammy of radiant and convective heat.[1] I pulled down the shroud from inside my helmet and covered as much of my face and neck as possible. Wildland PPE is "fire resistant," but it doesn't protect you from this kind of heat as well as our structural turnouts. We were

---

1 Convective heat is the transfer of heat from warm objects to cooler ones by the movement of air or water molecules that have been heated. Radiant heat is given off from warm objects in the form of invisible electromagnetic energy that is then absorbed by cooler objects.

struggling to hold our position because of the heat. I'm sure that if we had been standing there without helmets and gloves, we would have been badly burned. It was the highest level of heat I had ever felt on a fire. It made us all step back more than a few steps. We were standing in the middle of a 15-foot-wide patch of asphalt driveway that wrapped around the house. The burning barn was 100 feet away. The swath of asphalt and about ten feet of well-manicured lawn separated us and the house from the flashing tall grass and gave us just enough space for an anchor point for our defense. Suddenly, a storm-like mass of wind-blown embers burst from the barn as the bales of stacked hay inside flashed off in a giant continuous roar. We turned our backs to the fire and placed our full attention on spraying down the siding and roof of the house to defeat the embers' attack.

When E92 arrived, their crew joined us on the side of the house with a 1 1/2 attack line. The Chief had assigned them to assist us. Don and the officer on E92 agreed that the best approach was wetting down the house with as much water as possible. The only part of their conversation I could hear over the roar of the fire was E92's officer yelling, "Don't hit the windows with a straight stream. It will break them!" Don turned to me and yelled sarcastically, "Ya think?"

Chief Cates had also asked for a structure fire response because the old farmhouse just south of us had caught fire. Engine 94 quickly arrived and soon entered the house in their bunker gear. We also heard over the radio that multiple spotfires were growing in the wheat and grass fields to the northwest. Those fires were over a half mile away, caused by the windblown embers from the cedar barns. Doug Bleaker, a SCFD9 Assistant Chief, had taken command of the units assigned to those fires. He had a couple of DNR rigs chasing the spotfires and knocking them down just after they popped up.

Because the fire had moved around the back of the house, the threat was decreased enough that we were reassigned to extend an attack line to some burning hay bales behind the farmhouse. The burning bales were threatening a small garage behind the house.

Engine 94 had extinguished the main fire inside the house, but the crew was struggling to hunt down the fire's extension up into the second floor. The house was constructed in the late 1800s. It was built with continuous wood framing from one floor to the next without any fire stops. It's called balloon framing. Balloon-framed houses are notorious for letting you think the fire is out when, in fact, it has traveled within the walls to the upper floors and attic. The crew on E94 was doing their due diligence and tracking down any signs of heat in the walls throughout the structure. By the time they found all of the fire, ripped open the walls and extinguished the fire, the house was a total loss.

Once we extinguished the large hay bales next to the garage, we redeployed to help Gary and Theo extend attack lines from E96. Their assignment was to overhaul the three barns that had burned down to their foundations. The barns no longer existed but the concrete slabs were full of burning debris: mostly old cars and large burning cedar timbers.

By 8:00 PM, the winds had started to die, and it began to rain. The scene fell eerily quiet, almost peaceful, disturbed only by the sounds of spraying water and idling fire trucks. The fire ground and surrounding fields were lit only by the red, blue, and white emergency lights of half a dozen fire trucks.

Jon, who was running WT96, eventually joined us. He had been all over the fire ground, providing water to B96, E92, E94, and the DNR crews working the spot fires. He was jazzed about it all. Jon loves fighting wildland fires.

I recently read the final Fire Investigation Report (provided by the Department of Natural Resources) for the fire. It was officially named The Peone North Fire. The investigators concluded that the fire was caused by a surge in the power lines running along the east side of North Peone Road. The power surge was caused by a wind-blown metal roofing panel on an outbuilding of a neighboring property. The panel had been blown off the roof onto overhead power lines. It caused a short in the power lines, which sent a surge of power along the wires in all directions. At a point just above the origin of the Peone North Fire, the power line had been repaired years ago by splicing two lines together. When the surge passed through this section of wire, the increased resistance of the splice created a short between the wire and the ground, igniting the dry wheat field. The blowing dust from the haboob gave the current a continuous path for the charged particles to flow from the wire to the ground. The report indicated a local farmhand and his son were harvesting the adjacent field and spotted the smoke. They called 911. Two other fires were started by the same power surge at different locations in the area, but neither grew as quickly as the Peone North Fire. Eventually, all the resources sent to those other two fires were reassigned to the Peone North Fire.

I often drive by the properties that burned that day in August. There's no longer any sign of the three barns and the old farmhouse. The burned-out structures have all been removed, and now the property contains only a few old vehicles and a travel trailer. The surrounding wheat fields that did not burn that day have been sold off in ten-acre lots to create a gated community of million-dollar homes. The community is called Peone Landing. The homes are all beautifully constructed and well maintained, but the few old-timers who still live in the area miss the seemingly endless rolling fields of wheat that were a hallmark of the prairie. I imagine someday soon, someone will buy the property that held those old cedar barns and build their dream home. I wonder if they'll ever know that back in the 1800s, it was someone else's dream.

In retrospect, it was a memorable fire for all of us. Afterward, Chief Cates called it a "career fire." He told us we'd probably never be on another fire that had such a combination of challenges or burned so hot and fast. It sounded like a reasonable prediction at the time, but if you've read my earlier chapters, you will remember that the Nightmare House was called a career fire by another chief. And for me, the Macmahan Fire was as much a career fire as any I've worked on. I guess that's one of the reasons I've lasted this long as a volunteer. Another career fire might be just around the corner. You just never know.

The volunteer crew at Station 96 in the winter of 2023. From left to right
are: Jon Amend, Don Shearer, Dan McCann, Gary Woollett, Matt Olinger,
and Gavin Duffy.

Engine 96 and Brush 96 are parked in a stubble field east of Station 96
in the summer of 2023. Engine 96 has since been retired after 22 years of
service. The background is Forker Ridge. My log home on Black Bear Lane,
which I describe in the book's opening chapter, is located on the other side
of the ridge directly behind E96.

Don Shearer and Gary Woollett on a structure fire in the middle of the night. They had just replaced their near-empty air bottles with full ones and were ready for another assignment.

A group of volunteers from Station 96 pose for a picture after stopping a field fire. From left to right are Gary Woollett, Matt Olinger, Whitey Wentz, and Dan McCann.

Engine 96 and Water Tender 96 during a porta-tank training operation. The firefighter in the picture is Nic Price, a volunteer for several years who left Station 96 to become a full-time wildland firefighter.

The Life Flight helicopter, usually called "the bird," is on the ground and ready to take a stroke patient to the nearest hospital. Brush 96 in the foreground was our brush truck for twenty years before we replaced it in 2023.

This fire in this metal building I describe in the chapter "The Christmas Fires." I took the picture minutes after we exited the building through the person door shown on the right.

This picture shows the origin of the Wellesley Fire that occurred in August, 2016. The fire quickly grew to over 200 acres and threatened dozens of homes and outbuildings.

Gary Woollett checks for lingering smoke and flames on the second floor of a structure fire in November of 2022.

A Fire Boss dumps its 500-gallon load of water to help us protect homes in District 4 in August of 2021. We were working a fire about 10 miles north of Station 96 and in District 4. We responded with both B96 and WT96 and were able to protect numerous homes and buildings.

A selfie I took at 1 AM after fighting the Macmahan Fire on August 5, 2015. I was more than tired.

Life Flight preparing to lift off with our patient from a trauma call in November of 2023. Gary Woollett stands by the open gate to ensure no one approaches the helicopter. The photo shows how skilled a pilot must be when they drop into small, sloped spaces to help us save a patient.

Jon Amend is partially hidden by the smoke while fighting the Williams Lake Fire in August of 2022 at 11 PM.

Chapter 15

Universal Precautions

Coronavirus-19 (COVID-19) hit Washington State in the late winter of 2019. Most of the early cases occurred in western Washington in King County. The first confirmed case in Spokane County was on February 20, 2020.

In early March 2020, the university administration where I worked decided that students would not be allowed to return to campus after spring break. All classes for the remainder of the spring semester would be conducted online. For many faculty, this created a logistical mess. Creating new materials and methods for online education on the fly was an enormous undertaking for most faculty, and many were unhappy. However, the decision was made, and everyone had to adapt and live with it. I welcomed the news because it would dovetail beautifully with my planned June retirement. I taught for 28 years on campus, and I was ready to leave.

It was an easy transition for me to teach online. In the fall of 2014, I committed to "flipping the classroom" in all my classes. Flipping the classroom can mean different things to different people because it can be done in several ways. My approach was to have students complete a short reading assignment (6-8 pages) and watch a 30-minute video of me presenting the same material *before* attending class. In the video, which I made sitting at my desk, I narrated my usual lecture-style PowerPoint slides. A small window at the bottom of the screen displayed a video of me while I narrated. I could also re-record over mistakes I might have made or incorporate other types of media. The software I used to do this is called Camtasia.

This approach allowed me to make 30-minute videos covering the same material usually covered in 50-minute lectures. This was because students always asked questions about older material or questions that demonstrated they had yet to do the required reading in typical 50-minute lectures. Consequently, it was always a challenge to cover all the material I intended to cover, and we (the class) frequently got behind the semester syllabus. The best part of having students watch my videos *before* class was that when students came into class, I had the entire 50 minutes of class to answer questions and do example problems. Because I had been doing these flipped courses since 2014, I had all the materials, technology, and experience to go online immediately. All we had to change was to use Skype for the "in-class" student questions and problems. It was easy to make the change, and now that I was teaching from home, I was more available to respond to calls at the fire station! Win-win!

Consequently, dealing with COVID-19 at the university was easy for me. Dealing with COVID-19 as a first responder was another thing altogether.

As first responders, we were issued additional PPE including disposable gowns, P100 half-mask respirators, and goggles. The administration in SCFD9 also issued new EMS standard operating procedures (SOP). In the new SOP, Dispatch would notify us to use "universal precautions" whenever a patient's symptoms included difficulty breathing, nausea, or fever, and on all echo calls (i.e., CPR). Universal precautions meant we had to wear a disposable gown, our P100 half-mask respirator, safety glasses, or goggles and be double-gloved before we made patient contact or entered the residence. This new SOP required the additional PPE for almost every severe EMS call. We also had to use universal precautions anytime we performed CPR (i.e., an "echo" call) because CPR dramatically increases the risks of aerosolizing the patient's exhaled air. It sounds straightforward, but it wasn't. Getting outfitted in gowns, goggles, and extra gloves had the potential to cause delays in making patient contact.

We dealt with these challenges by designating one of our crew as a "runner." A runner would gown up while we were driving to the scene, carry a portable radio, and quickly make patient contact inside the residence. They asked the patient a few key questions and took their temperature. The questions were about travel history, difficulty breathing, presence of fever, and possible exposures to people diagnosed with COVID-19. The runner would then use the portable radio to update the crews outside and decide if universal precautions were, in fact, necessary for everyone. Using a runner consequently decreased the number of people exposed to COVID-19.

A designated runner worked best when we responded with three or more people in the truck. But in reality, we responded 95% of the time with only two people: a driver and an officer. This meant neither of us could gown up while driving to the scene. Consequently, making patient contact usually took a few more precious minutes.

Matt, who lived across the street from the station, would occasionally arrive early enough to gown up before anyone else showed up. But, if Matt was unavailable, whoever drove didn't have the time to gown up before responding.

When Captain Don and I responded together, I was always the one assigned to patient care and served as the runner. Consequently, the first few minutes on the scene of any Charlie, delta, or echo call had me scrambling into a gown, getting double-gloved, and donning my respirator and glasses. Before entering the residence, I also had to grab a radio, the basic life support (BLS) medical bag, and the Automated Electrical Defibrillator (AED). Once with the patient, I'd handle the first five minutes or so of the call alone. It was a challenge, especially if I had to climb a flight or two of steep stairs to get to the patient. Sometimes, when I finally got to the patient, I was more breathless than they were!

When I think about being a first responder during COVID-19, the most consistent image I have in my mind is me or someone else hustling into a house wearing a white or blue disposable gown. The following two calls might be to blame for that memorable image.

It was early on a Monday evening, January 11, 2021. We received an echo call for a 25-year-old male on Morrison Road. Matt and Don were first at the station. Matt had gowned up and was sitting in the driver's seat of B96 when Don climbed into the officer's seat. The address was a mile from the station.

As they headed north on Forker Road, Don radioed Dispatch they were responding. Dispatch gave the update, "We have a 25-year-old male in full arrest. His girlfriend is on the scene and has begun CPR. He was released from the hospital three days ago for a fractured vertebra in his back, and he told his girlfriend on the phone that he had been experiencing a lot of pain from his injury and was taking prescribed painkillers."

When the girlfriend arrived home from work, she found him unconscious on the floor in the kitchen, called 911, and began CPR.

As I arrived at the station in my side-by-side, I could see B96 turning onto Morrison Road. I drove past the station and headed directly to the scene.

When I turned south on Morrison and crested a small hill in the road, I could see B96 heading up the driveway. I followed them in and parked off the driveway in a field. Just then, Jon pulled up behind me in his Suburban. Engine 94 and Valley Engine 5 (VE5) also rolled in behind us. It was dark, but all the emergency lights illuminated the scene.

I caught a quick glimpse of Matt entering the house, all gowned up. Don was helping Mark, who had also come POV, into his gown. I ran over to B96 and grabbed a set of PPE. Mark headed for the door, and Don helped me get gowned as quickly as possible. While heading for the front door of the daylight basement where Matt had entered, I saw someone from E94 in a gown heading in the door as well.

When Matt entered the house, he found the patient's girlfriend doing what he later described as "pretty darn good CPR." As he approached her, he said, "You're doing great. Keep it up, and I'll take over in a minute."

Matt cut off the patient's shirt, pulled out a set of AED pads, applied them to the patient, turned on the AED, and asked the girl to pause compressions. He felt for a carotid pulse. Nothing.

"I've got CPR," he said and took over.

The next people who came into the room included Mark, Chris, the designated runner from E94, me, and Jon. The patient was still in the kitchen, where he had fallen, and it was getting crowded. Chris said to everyone, "We need to move him into the living room."

Without another word, people were sliding furniture and med bags out of the way and moving him into the middle of the room.

The room soon filled with other first responders, including Sam, the medic from E94. Sam announced he was the medic in charge and running the code. Dan Ash, the officer on E94 (also a medic), slid in next to me and started an IV. Soon, the patient was intubated.

Matt, Mark, Jon, and I all began working on the patient with the medics. We each took shifts doing compressions and ventilations, holding the IV bag, and monitoring the femoral pulse. Sam was calm and collected as he ran the code. As soon as the IV was established, Dan started administering the usual rounds of cardiac drugs.

During the standard Pit Crew CPR[2] protocol, a brief pause is built into the sequences of compressions and ventilations to assess if a shockable rhythm

---

2 Pit Crew CPR designates anywhere from 3 to 7 specific roles during CPR, depending on the number of available first responders. A quick Internet search will yield more than you want to know about the process.

is present. Repeatedly, the Life Pack monitor showed the patient's heart had no electrical activity. He was in a sustained asystole.

With compression and ventilations well established and the standard cardiac drugs on board, Sam administered a dose of Narcan. A few minutes later, he went with a second dose. I was on the femoral artery, and after the second dose, I suddenly felt a pulse and told Sam, "I've got a pulse!" Things were looking up.

We maintained CPR for another two minutes. Sam called a pause for analysis of the ECG. Sure enough, the ECG was back and in a sinus rhythm. A carotid pulse was also present.

Within a few minutes, the patient started breathing independently and blinked his eyes. Sam removed the intubation tube. Once the tube was out, the patient opened his eyes. You could see the confusion on his face, so Sam slowly explained that his heart had stopped, and we revived him.

His first words were, "Man, my chest is killing me."

Matt responded, "Your girlfriend did that to you."

We all laughed. It was a laugh of relief more than anything else. That little laugh felt damn good.

Within ten minutes, the patient sat up and told Sam what he could remember about the number and timing of pain meds he had taken. Based on his prescription and what he told Sam, he had mistakenly taken more than prescribed. He also had a few beers. The mystery of his collapse was solved.

During all this, Jon had taken the girlfriend outside to give her some space and time to regain her composure. He brought her back in to see him when he was told the patient was alert and talking. All she could do was cry and give him a long hug. I hope she'll eventually have more to say to him about the whole thing. After all, she saved his ass, and I'm guessing she'll explain that to him in no uncertain terms. At least, I hope so.

Looking around the room, I saw Don and Gavin standing in the back, watching everything. There were also a few crew members from VE5. I was surprised by how many people were in the room. It's amazing how focused you get on a call like this. It certainly makes you live in the moment.

As I looked around, everyone was starting to clean up the mess of medical equipment, discarded plastic packages, and biohazard bags; I noticed that everyone who was gowned, wearing respirators, gloves, and glasses, was almost unrecognizable as individuals. But the group had been a great team. Standing there looking around, I felt satisfied for being part of it.

As we each walked out of the house, we gathered in a group and began to peel off our PPE carefully. The goal was to do it as prescribed in training so we didn't contaminate ourselves while placing everything in biohazard bags. You could see the relief on everyone's face as they got out of the hot garments. The cold January evening wind chilled our sweat-covered skin almost immediately. The group broke up as the cold January wind forced us to return to our trucks and retrieve our coats and hats. It was time to head home.

The call had been one of our first echo calls during COVID-19. It was a great success. But for me, the white gowns and respirators gave it a different look and feel from the echo calls I'd been a part of pre-COVID-19. I wondered if it was a brief view into the future: a future when new viruses and unintentional overdoses increasingly put us all at risk. I hope not, but I believe it was.

The second echo call that comes to mind during the peak days of the pandemic was about five months later.

It was a hot and sunny June day, and the call was a 31D. The address was on North Norman Road, four miles from the station. Norman Road is on the far side of the ridge east of the station. The drive's last three miles are on tight, twisty gravel roads. It's a 10-minute response time, and adding the five minutes it takes me to get from my house to the driver's seat of B96, plus the time to gown up, makes it at least 18 minutes before I make patient contact. All this went through my mind as I navigated the dips and curves through the woods in my RZR side-by-side.

As usual, Captain Don was waiting for me when I arrived, and we were immediately off in B96 with lights and sirens. When Don signed on the radio, Dispatch gave us the short. Our patient had called 911 and was alone at home. He was an adult male with severe difficulty breathing. He'd given Dispatch the gate code for his driveway gate. Soon after, Dispatch lost all communication with him; they recommended "universal precautions."

Engine 92 was en route, and their medic had given dispatch the command to launch Life Flight. An ALS ambulance from AMR was also responding. Don and I knew we'd get on the scene well before E92 and the AMR unit. I would be the runner and get inside as quickly as possible.

When we pulled up to the driveway, we couldn't find the keypad to open the gate. Don immediately climbed over the gate and used a keypad on the inside of the gate to open it. I drove through the gate, but Don couldn't find a way to lock the gate open, so he just jumped in with me, and we headed up the steep hill to the house, which was about 50 yards up the driveway. We climbed out at the house, and Don helped me gown up. I donned my respirator, gloves, and glasses, grabbed the AED and BLS bag, and headed for the front door.

I found the patient as soon as I entered the house. He was a large male, certainly 250 pounds or more, lying prone and shirtless about 10 feet from the front door. The interior of the house felt unusually warm. I dropped all my gear and checked his carotid for a pulse. He was in full arrest.

I keyed the microphone on my radio and called Don, "Brush 96, full arrest!"

"Copy, full arrest," replied Don.

I started CPR, knowing everyone was coming, and now they understood our delta call was an echo call.

When the ambulance arrived at the locked gate, Don was hurrying to gown up. He ran down the driveway and let them in. Just then, Life Flight started circling the house, and E92 called Don on the radio to tell him they would not arrive in time to find a landing zone (LZ) for the bird. They told Don he would have to do it.

As Life Flight circled, Don picked a possible LZ just inside the front yard and asked Life Flight to have a look. It was on the small side, about 75 feet in diameter. The pilot said it would be fine.

Just then, E92 pulled up. Tom was the officer on E92, and he told Don to head back up to the house, and he'd land the bird.

I had been alone in the house doing CPR for what seemed an eternity when the gowned-up ambulance crew came through the door. The medic and EMT started prepping the patient with their Life Pack 1500, AED, and bag-valve-mask resuscitator (BVM). I was sweating profusely, sweat was dripping from my forehead onto the inside of my safety glasses, and I was breathing hard through my respirator from the effort.

"I'm gonna need a break soon," I said to no one in particular.

The AMR crew didn't respond. They were busy, and I continued for another minute or more.

"I'm gonna need a break," I said more loudly.

I was starting to struggle to get the depth I needed with my compressions. The patient had a large muscular chest, and I used my body weight to get the two-plus inches of depth on each compression. My wrists, arms, and back were starting to ache. I'm sure I had been doing compressions for ten minutes or more.

"I can switch with you," the EMT finally said.

"Great," I replied.

My first thought was that she looked small and would have problems giving effective compressions. But I was fading fast. She'd probably be just fine. She'd have to be.

She slipped in next to me, and I passed compressions over to her. She didn't miss a beat. I took over manual ventilations with the BVM.

Just then, others started coming in to help. Soon, even the flight crew from Life Flight was participating in our standard Pit Crew CPR protocol. In a few minutes, I could finally stand up and step back as different people rotated into the crew. The house once again felt extremely hot and stifling. I needed some fresh air badly.

I walked out of the house, into the yard, and removed my respirator. The fresh air immediately made me feel better. I was dripping with sweat and could feel my shirt sticking to my back. Jeff, the SCFD9 EMS Director, walked past me towards the house and nodded. I just nodded back.

Unfortunately, the crews inside could not get a return of spontaneous circulation (ROSC). The crew worked on him for 45 minutes before the medic called it. There was nothing else we could do.

As we started picking up our gear, the patient's live-in girlfriend approached the house. I'm not sure if someone called her or she arrived unexpectedly. The picture I have in my mind is seeing her sitting on the lawn in the shade of a large tree while Tom, the officer from E92, sat and talked with her. She looked to be in shock.

Since that day, I can still picture her as we drive past that residence on our way to other calls on North Norman Road. She's always sitting there under that tree, alone. Sometimes, I see images of myself alone in the house doing CPR on her boyfriend. I'm dressed in a white gown, blue gloves, a respirator, and dark safety glasses, doing endless compressions. It's a haunting vision of what COVID-19 did to far too many.

These two stories don't scratch the surface of the many times we had to follow universal precaution guidelines on our calls. But, when I think of being a first responder during COVID-19, these calls immediately come to mind. They represent the two extremes of my experience, one good and one not. I can't imagine what it must have been like for first responders in places like New York City. Hopefully, the next time, which is inevitable, we'll be better prepared.

Chapter 16

The Christmas Fires

Christmas fires are something people do not want to think about because of their potential for disaster and heartbreak. Dry trees, piles of wrapping paper and cardboard boxes piled underneath, lit candles scattered about the room, hot lights illuminated all day and night wrapped around it all, and a bounty of holiday cheer spell Christmas disaster in capital letters. Fortunately, Christmas fires have been few and far between during my time at Station 96.

The first Christmas fire I experienced occurred on December 25, 2002. At 9:00 PM, my pager went off for an 11F on North Judkins Lane, about a half mile from my house. I lived on Black Bear Lane back then, and my first intention was to drive POV to the address. But, by the time I was headed up my driveway, I decided I should head straight to Station 96. Going to a structure fire without PPE or tools is seldom a good move. Besides, both E96 and WT96 were on the call, and I wasn't sure enough folks to staff both rigs would respond on Christmas Eve.

Station 96 was about four miles from home, and as I described in earlier chapters, the road to the station was challenging. The early part of the trip was particularly difficult because it contained many downhill tight left and right turns. On this Christmas Eve, the roads were covered in hard-packed snow with a topcoat of ice.

As I headed down from the ridge, I almost put my SUV in the ditch multiple times. I was increasingly worried our fire trucks might not get to the fire. As I reached the bottom of Judkins Road, I could see E96 approaching. I slowed to a stop and flashed my lights, hoping they would stop so I could warn them of the road conditions.

We had gotten a new E96 that past summer. It was four-wheel drive (the only one in the district) and had "on-spots" (automated chains) on the rear inner wheels. I figured if anyone made it to the fire, it would be E96. But I still wanted to warn them.

Brian, our Training Lieutenant at the time, was driving, and he slowed to a stop, guessing it was me flashing my lights. Captain Mike was in the officer's seat. Don and Whitey were in the back seats.

When we both stopped, I yelled to Brian, "It's ice all the way up."

"Oh great," said Brain sarcastically.

"I'll go grab the tender," I yelled.

"Copy that," Brian replied.

I was later told that as Brian and I drove away in different directions, Mike asked Brian, "Did he say it was all OK?"

"He said it was all ice," Brian replied.

"Oh shit," was all Mike said.

I'm guessing Don and Whitey were thinking something similar as they continued donning their SCBAs in the back seats. Maybe they were too busy to care.

Once I turned north on Forker Road, I realized it was all black ice. I drove as fast as I dared, about 25 mph. Water Tender 96 was a 1,500-gallon four-wheel drive tender built in 1980. It was a 4-speed manual and slow as molasses. I knew it was not chained up, so as I crawled along, I hoped there was someone else already at the station chaining it up.

I had brought my radio scanner with me when I left the house, and I heard the short from Dispatch to all incoming units. The 911 caller from the residence told Dispatch the house was slowly filling with smoke, but there was no apparent fire. The residents were evacuating. I also learned that E94, WT94, E92, and 920 were responding.

When I arrived at the station, Gary was getting into his turnouts. I told him, "The road to Judkins Lane is all ice. We need to chain up the tender."

"Yeah. So's my driveway and Scribner Road. The canyon's all black ice," he replied with little enthusiasm.

As we wrestled with the heavy chains while lying under the tender's rear wheel, we could hear the radio traffic over the station radio. Neither E92 nor E94 had taken the time to put on their chains, and now E92 was stuck on the steepest part of Moffat Road. They started sliding backwards as they lost traction had almost slid off the road. E94 was similarly stuck on Judkins Road, about a half mile higher than where I had earlier met E96. Engine 94 was parked on the icy hill, and the crew were all scrambling to put their chains on the rear wheels. It sounded bad, very bad.

Soon, Gary and I were headed south on Forker at 25 mph. As we turned east on Judkins Road, we came upon WT94. They were slowly climbing the hill, passing the stranded E94. Station 94's water tender was new. It had on-spots and twin lockable rear axles. Those traction devices and the 24,000 pounds of water they carried gave them just enough traction to climb the hill.

As we chugged up the hill past E94, we could see Lieutenant Lobdell standing but sliding down the road beside the engine. He was frantically grabbing for handholds he could use to keep from falling. We waved and soldiered on.

"They should've chained up," Gary and I said simultaneously. It made us both laugh, but it was a nervous laugh.

As we climbed Judkins Road, Captain Mike called Dispatch. "Dispatch. Engine 96 is on the scene. We have a one-story residence with nothing showing. Several of the residents are standing outside. This will be Judkins Command."

When Gary and I arrived about 10 min later, we parked behind WT94, climbed out, waved to the guys sitting in WT94, and followed the charged attack line from E96 up to the back of the house. The attack line was lying outside the slider door leading to the kitchen. Steve, the homeowner, met us at the door and told me the guys from E96 were all inside. Steve said he thought the fire was in the wall or attic and probably caused by an electrical short. He had found a tripped circuit breaker in his electrical box, and there was a slight smell of melting wire insulation before the room started to fill with smoke. I asked about his wife, Rosemary, and their kids, and he told us they were all sitting in their Chevy Suburban. The big SUV was parked in the yard and running with the heater on to keep them warm.

All the lights in the house were on. We found Mike and Brian in the living room. They had cleared most of the smoke by opening several windows. Whitey and Don had their SCBAs on and were setting up our small aluminum attic ladder to access the attic space from the hallway. Whitey went up first as Don passed him the water can, a pressurized fire extinguisher filled with water. Then Don followed him up into the attic. Our 920 Officer, Chief Van Heal, arrived, and Mike briefed him.

Whitey and Don quickly found a small insulation fire near a junction box in the attic and extinguished the burning insulation. Gary and I grabbed a tarp from E96, brought it in, and laid it on the floor to gather the burnt insulation. When this was done, they double-checked the attic and climbed down, convinced the fire was out. Mike and Chief Van Heal canceled E94 and WT94. Engine 92 had notified 920 that they were out of service and waiting for a tow truck.

Captain Mike talked with Steve, the homeowner, about what we found and told him not to reenergize that circuit breaker until after an electrician checked out the situation. Steve told Mike he had personally done all the electrical work when he built the house about five years ago. I think he was feeling a bit embarrassed. We told him it was unlikely his fault and there was no reason to worry about it tonight anyway.

"Just be sure to call us if you smell or see any more smoke," I told him. Try to enjoy Christmas Eve.

We picked up all our gear, loaded the trucks, and headed back down to Forker Road. About halfway down the icy road, we got a call from Dispatch. Steve had called 911 again because he saw and smelled faint light gray smoke in the living room. Mike told Brian to turn E96 around and head back to the house. We were farther down the hill than E96 and decided to stage WT96 on Judkins Road to be sure they needed us before climbing the icy hill a second time.

When Mike and his E96 crew returned to the house, he radioed us and asked us to bring the tender back up to the house just to be safe. Chief Van Heal also returned to the house.

A search of the attic established that the original fire was out. However, smoke was coming from below the attic in a seam where the interior wall joined the attic space. A small amount of smoldering insulation had fallen into the interior wall space. We had no choice but to cut out a four-by-eight section of sheetrock from the wall in the living room to remove the smoldering insulation.

We cleared all the smoke from the house and decided to wait at least 30 more minutes before packing up and heading down the hill. It was now 1:00 AM.

No more smoke appeared, and we were back in the station by about 2:00 AM. We all felt a bit bad about missing that smoldering piece of insulation. But the fact is, we got there soon enough to stop what would have eventually been a full-fledged structure fire on Christmas Eve. Something none of us wanted to see.

The year after the fire, Steve, Rosemary, and the kids showed up unexpectedly at Station 96 during our Tuesday night drill the week before Christmas. Rosemary had made us a batch of cookies and treats, and they thanked us repeatedly for saving their home. It was a heartwarming experience for all of us. I think of it each Christmas Eve and smile. But it also makes me wonder what might be lurking in the walls of our house or my neighbors' houses.

It was 18 years later, on Christmas Day, 2020, when my pager went off for another Christmas fire. When I looked up at the clock, it was 4:35 AM. I climbed out of bed and headed for our walk-in closet to get dressed. Putting on my reading glasses, I scrolled through the pager. It was a structure fire (11F) on North Canwell Road in District 4. However, Spokane County Fire District 4 (SCFD4) has limited resources that can reach that area in under 1/2 hour. Consequently, they have been given permission by SCFD9 to add WT96 to their structure fires. It's not uncommon that we send other resources as well. I could see on my phone from the station text chain that Matt was on his way to the station. I decided to go, thinking he might want company in the tender.

As I hustled my RZR through the dark woods, I hoped it would be a false alarm. Arriving at the station, I found Mark and Whitey had arrived a minute earlier. Matt had already left in the tender.

Matt later told us that before he left with WT96, he called District 4's 420 Officer on the radio. The conversation went like this.

"420, this is tender 96."

"Go for 420 Tender 96," he replied.

"We have a crew to staff E96 if you'd like to add E96," Matt said.

"Yeah, add E96."

Consequently, Mark, Whitey, and I were standing in the turnout room when we got added to the call by Dispatch. We were scrambling into our turnouts as Gary came through the station door.

"Do they just want the tender?" he asked.

"Matt's already gone in the tender. They just added E96," I replied.

Soon, we rolled out the door lights and sirens. I was driving, Gary was in the officer's seat, Mark and Whitey were in the back and donning their SCBAs.

The address of the fire was on North Canwell Road, which is about 6

1/2 miles from Station 96. We figured Matt would be the first resource on the scene, and we were anxious to get his size up. He did get there first, but Canwell Road branches off Bill-Gulch Road and heads straight uphill. Matt was afraid if he drove up there in the tender, he might have nowhere to turn around or park out of the way of the incoming engines, so he began to hike up the hill to the address. About three-quarters of the way up the hill, Engine 44 (E44) showed up and drove past him straight to the fire.

When E44 got on the scene, they called in their size-up.

"Dispatch, Engine 44 is on the scene. We've got a 40 by 80 metal building with smoke showing from the eves in the back. Engine 44 will be Canwell Command and initiate an offensive attack."

Command told Matt he had plenty of room for the tender, so Matt drove the tender up the hill and set up a tender nurse (direct transfer of water from the tender to the engine using a single three-inch diameter hose) with E44.

Now we knew we had a real fire, not a false alarm. We arrived just minutes after E44, and Command told us to break into two crews. The first crew would assist E44's attack at the back of the building. Gary and Whitey took that assignment as 96-bravo. Mark and I were assigned to attempt to gain access from the front of the building as 96-alpha.

When Gary and Whitey arrived at the back of the building, they discovered that only one firefighter from E44 was on the attack line. More troublesome was that E44 had parked too far from the building, and the 200-foot attack line only made it to the corner of the building. This prevented them from making a full attack on the fire. In addition, they laid the attack line along the building under a shed roof. This made the hoseline vulnerable to fire, especially if the shed roof collapsed, which ultimately it did. Gary and Whitey then had to shut down the hoseline and used additional hoses from Engine 46 (E46), which had just arrived, to replace the line. The assignment for E46 was to put out spot fires on the neighboring property and prevent a seven-foot-high vinyl fence from melting.

As Gary and Whitey worked at the rear of the building, Mark and I attempted to gain access from the front of the building. There were two metal overhead 12 by 15-foot garage doors and a single person door for access. Both overhead doors were locked, but the person door was not, so that would be our access point.

Mark and I pulled a 200-foot attack line from E44, called for water, and radioed Command that we were entering the building through the alpha-side person door.

We donned our masks and started to enter by crawling on hands and knees, dragging the charged attack line, and carrying forcible entry tools. We were engulfed in thick smoke as soon as we entered the building.

When a room or building fills with smoke, it first fills the ceiling area because hot air and gas rise. Then, as it accumulates in the room, it fills down to the floor. But in our case, the smoke and gases were already down to the floor, and we couldn't see our hands in front of our faces. I immediately radioed Command.

"Canwell command, 96-alpha," I called.

"Go for command 96-alpha."

"We have entered the alpha side and have zero visibility with smoke down to the floor. We need those overhead doors vented."

"Copy, ventilate the overhead doors," was Command's reply.

It was also apparent that the room we entered was closed off to the rest of the building because we couldn't see the glow from the fire or feel its heat. Mark led with the nozzle and immediately bumped into several obstacles blocking his path. He tried to go left and then right with no luck. The room was stuffed full of furniture.

I grabbed Mark by the shoulder and yelled in his ear as the sound of the fire grew louder.

"Mark, we're backing out. Now!"

"Copy that," Mark replied.

We backed out of the building and turned to see a firefighter chopping a large hole in the left-side overhead door. As we pulled our hoseline back from the building, heavy smoke started to billow from the eves of the entire building. I turned to look through the gaping hole in the overhead door. There was nothing to see but fire. It was like looking into a red-hot coal furnace.

In the back of the building, Gary and Whitey were flooding the interior of the building through a large window that had shattered from the heat. After that single hole was cut in the front overhead door, a massive flame leaped from the window and washed over their heads.

The 3,000-square-foot shop flashed over as the tremendous volume of unburnt gases trapped in the building received the needed oxygen. It was a stunning thing to watch, a classic spontaneous reaction of rapid oxidation that I had first learned about in high school chemistry. The building and everything in it were going to burn to the ground. There was nothing we could do about it.

Mark and I pulled back from the building and watched it burn. Within a minute, we could see the room we had been in filled wall to wall, floor to ceiling, with raging fire. We were no longer in an offensive fire attack. We had no choice but to transition into a defensive fire attack and manage the burning building. Mark later told me that seeing that room suddenly flash over with fire made him realize we would have been severely burned if not killed if we had stayed there. I felt the same way.

We started to cool off the outside of the building to prevent the fire from spreading to the brush and trees surrounding the shop. But every time we'd fully open our nozzle, Gary would report a loss of water pressure at the back of the building. Something wasn't right with the water supply.

We discovered that when Matt established his tender nurse with E44, the E44 operator had not engaged E44's pump. Consequently, Matt's pump in WT96 supplied flow and pressure through the pump in E44 and then directly to Gary's attack line. Therefore, the overall draw was too great when we opened our attack lines, and the pressure dropped. Eventually, Matt and the operator on E44 got E44's pump engaged, and we had plenty of water and pressure. But the issue made us realize that if we were still in the building when it flashed over, we would have lost our water pressure defending ourselves from the flames. Deciding to leave that building when we did just might have been the smartest (or luckiest) thing I've ever done on a fire.

It took several hours for the shop to burn down, and we all pulled back to the trucks at one point because a large amount of ammunition was going off inside the shop. This is not uncommon in rural communities like ours, and I've been on more fires than I can name where rounds started going off in burning houses, garages, and outbuildings. Unfortunately, this kind of thing happens at structure fires all over the country, and a simple Internet search is all it takes to find numerous examples of firefighters getting seriously injured by exploding ammunition. It's a hazard our PPE isn't designed to mitigate.

Hours later, Command decided he could release E96 and WT96 from the fire. It was about 9:30 AM when we got back to Station 96. It was a Christmas morning I'll never forget.

Eventually, we discovered the cause of the fire was arson. The shopowner was away on vacation, and someone who had issues with him drove up to the shop in the early morning of Christmas Day and set it on fire.

I believe it's true that one's lack of intelligence might best be judged by one's actions. Or, as Forest Gump said so eloquently. "Stupid is as stupid does."

Chapter 17

Empathy and Compassion

Fires can be devastating to people and their families. Even if no one is physically injured, a fire can change a person's life forever. As firefighters, we seldom know what happens to the people we see as they watch their homes, and everything in it goes up in smoke and flames. This is a story about the first time these thoughts took hold in my mind. Since that day, they have never left. Yet, I have learned that empathy and compassion can be, like all things, subject to change.

It was about twenty-five years ago, deep into October when my pager went off for an 11F on East Scribner Road. I don't remember the date or exact time, but I know I was living on Black Bear Lane and had to make the four-mile drive to Station 96. It was early in the morning, just about dawn, and the sky held the promise of snow.

Lieutenant Brian and Whitey were the first two volunteers to arrive at the station. They climbed into their turnouts and headed out in our 1980 four-wheel-drive E96. The engine held 500 gallons of water, had a 750-gallon-per-minute pump, and three attack lines. It was as slow as molasses. When I drove this truck for my official driving test back in 1996, I accidentally snapped the driveshaft in half by giving it too much throttle in first gear on a steep hill. I was happy to see it replaced in 2000.

When I arrived at the station, Don was waiting. We piled into our 1980 International four-wheel drive 1,500-gallon WT96. Both E96 and WT96 were painfully slow, painted green, and had manual transmissions. They were difficult to drive, but once we got on the scene, they could be effective.

When Brian and Whitey arrived at the bottom of Scribner Road, they headed east up towards the ridge. The address was about an eighth of a mile up the road, but they missed the driveway, driving past it. Don and I were next to arrive at Scribner. As we turned east onto Scribner, E92 was soon right behind us.

A short distance up Scribner, Don yelled, "Stop, stop here!"

"What's wrong?" I asked.

"That's the driveway back there, we missed it."

I stopped in the middle of the road. Engine 92 immediately called us on the radio.

"WT96, why have you stopped? We can't get around you."

"We just passed the driveway. We need to back up." Don told them.

Once both trucks backed up, we headed up the driveway.

Smartphones and Google Maps hadn't been invented back then, so all of our navigation depended on either local knowledge or being able to read a county map book while bouncing along gravel roads in the dark.

The driveway had three address posts, so we were not surprised when we soon came to a three-way intersection. The smoke and orange glow in the trees told us the house was straight ahead. However, we hesitated because we weren't sure if there was room for both us and E92 up at the house. Don told me to pull into the driveway on the left and waved E92 past us so they could drive straight to the fire.

Immediately, we saw a local resident walking down the driveway we had parked on. Don was surprised to see that it was Gary Woollett, someone he had known for years. Gary explained how his next-door neighbor had headed into town to his favorite watering hole the previous night and left his wood stove burning to keep his single-wide trailer warm. He returned after last call to find his trailer was on fire. He then ran over to Gary's house and began banging on the front door. Gary and his wife, Theresa, had been awakened minutes earlier by the sound of gunfire coming from the burning trailer. Gary called 911. As time would tell, it was this brief discussion between Don and Gary in the predawn light that helped Gary decide it was time he became a volunteer at Station 96. He joined up later that year.

When E92 arrived at the fire, they called Dispatch with their size-up.

"Dispatch. Engine 92 is on the scene. We have a single-wide trailer that's fully involved. Engine 92 will be Scribner Command."

Command then called us and told us there was room for us to come up the driveway to the house, so we headed up to the fire scene and parked next to E92. We quickly set up a tender nurse operation to serve as a water supply and extended an attack line so we could help put water on the burning trailer. Unfortunately, there was little we could do, which is too often the case when single-wide trailers catch fire. The trailer was "on the ground," a phrase that means the structure has collapsed and become more of a pile of burning trash than a trailer or a home.

The rest of the morning would be a slow process of drowning the burning debris pile and carefully pulling it apart to get underneath the metal roof and metal siding that covered what was left of the trailer and its contents. This process is called "overhaul." It's a dirty, tiring, dangerous, and toxic job.

Our 920 Officer, as well as E94 and E96, had arrived on the scene several minutes after we did. The 920 Officer was Chief Grau. I'd only met Chief Grau a couple of times at that point in my career, and I found him to be irritable and humorless. He soon sent E94 and E96 back in service, leaving the overhaul work to E92 and WT96.

The fire was still very hot, and occasionally, we heard ammunition popping off from within the debris pile. The homeowner had enough weapons and ammunition in the trailer that we decided to wait until the ammo stopped exploding before addressing the remaining burning mess.

As we waited, I noticed an elderly gentleman sitting alone on a small rock wall at the edge of the clearing surrounding the burning trailer. He was wearing a beat-up old cowboy hat, sitting with his head between his hands, staring down at the ground, and smoking a cigarette. I walked over to him. Dawn had arrived, but it was overcast, gray, and cold. It looked like it was about to snow.

"Sir, was this your home?" I asked.

He looked up at me with bloodshot, watery eyes and nodded yes. I thought he was still quite drunk.

"I'm very sorry for your loss. Is there someone you can call so you can get out of the cold?"

He just stared at the ground.

I didn't know what else to say, so I walked over to Chief Grau and told him the situation. He was writing in a notebook and just nodded without looking up at me. I walked away, found the officer on E92, and explained the situation. He told me not to worry; he'd handle it. He walked over to talk with the homeowner.

It took us a couple more hours to pull all the metal off the burned-out trailer and soak the remains with all the water we had. By the time we were done, it was just a stinking mass of hot metal and ash. It then began snowing very lightly, which I took as a message it was time to head home. Don and I were the last to head back to the station.

Twenty years ago, we didn't wear SCBAs during overhaul. As I write this story, I can only imagine the long list of carcinogenic compounds we probably inhaled that morning. Nothing was rewarding in the work, but it had to be done. Now that it was, I was glad it was over. Over the years, I have sometimes thought about the old man I talked to that day. As I stated at the beginning of this story, fires can be devastating for the people involved. When we left that cold, gray morning to clean up our truck and go back to Station 96, I wondered what would become of him. How would he rebuild his life? Would he?

I later learned that the homeowner eventually purchased a double-wide home from Dan Howard, one of Station 96's long-time volunteers, who is now retired. Dan's old double-wide was moved to the Scribner address to replace the burned-out trailer. Soon, the old man was living there with his daughter and mother.

Over the next ten years, we returned to that residence several times. Once, it was to put the homeowner's daughter, who was in labor, into an ambulance to get her to the hospital. Her water had broken, and the only action she could get from her father was that he called a cab for her. She rightly decided that a cab was too little, too late, and called 911. While we were at the house, the homeowner sat in the living room, drinking beer, smoking, and watching a football game. He was utterly uninterested in the whole thing. It was one of those dumbfounding moments for me, to be sure.

The next time we were there, it was for the homeowner's sick mother. She was elderly and bedridden. I don't remember what her primary complaint was. I do, however, remember helping to put her on a backboard and pass her through her bedroom window because it was the most practical way to get her out of the house. Once again, the homeowner sat in the living room, drinking beer, smoking, and watching TV.

A few years later, we were called to respond because a child had been bitten by a dog. Don, Gary and I arrived, and for some reason, I remember making sure my turnout coat was zipped up and I had my heavy gloves on. I'm a dog person, so I'm comfortable around dogs. But I had a bad feeling about this residence, and I was going in prepared for anything.

When I entered the house, there was a large pregnant Great Dane and a smaller dog in the living room. I asked the child's mother which of the two dogs had bitten the child. She told me it was the small dog. I asked her to move both dogs into a bedroom. She did as I asked, and I attended to the child. She had a bleeding puncture on her left cheek that we swabbed and cleaned. When E92 showed up, we brought them up to speed and passed patient care over to their medic. They eventually sent the child to the hospital in the ambulance for further evaluation.

The Sheriff and Animal Control showed up, and I told them what the mom had told me. Eventually, however, the mom admitted to the Sheriff that it was the Great Dane that had bitten the child. I don't know why she lied to me. Perhaps she was afraid the authorities might classify the pregnant Great Dane as a danger and take it from them. If that happened, they would lose the potential income from selling the puppies. Or maybe she thought I'd be less intimidated by the small dog. I have no idea. It hit me as one more example of strange behavior in a strange house. In any event, we left it to the Sheriff and Animal Control to work it all out.

There was at least one more call to that residence a few years ago that Gary and Matt had recently told me about. The call came in as a 31D, with difficulty breathing. The homeowner was the patient. He was at home, smoking a cigarette and wearing a nose cannula, flowing three liters of oxygen per minute. The medics decided he needed to go to the hospital, and he reluctantly agreed to go. When they told him to put out his cigarette, he became irritated and verbally abusive. He eventually got in the ambulance, and off they went. Gary told me he didn't survive long enough to return home. He was just one more example of someone with advanced COPD who couldn't stop smoking. Thinking back to the day his single-wide trailer burned to the ground, I still remember my intense feelings of empathy and compassion toward the homeowner. But, in truth, when I consider what we've experienced at that address over the years, it's the kids growing up there, not the homeowner, that get my empathy and compassion. That's the best I can do.

<h1 style="text-align:center">Chapter 18</h1>

<h1 style="text-align:center">The Wellesley Fire</h1>

On August 21, 2016, red flag warnings were in place in Spokane County. When the Wellesley Fire started at 2:30 PM, the temperature was 91 degrees, RH was 13%, and the winds were out of the southwest at a steady 24 mph. Wind gusts were consistently over 30 mph.

The earliest recorded 911 call reporting the fire was at 2:48 PM. The caller reported smoke in the distance while traveling eastbound along Interstate 90 from approximately seven miles away. A second 911 caller, also at 2:48 PM, reported the fire was in the Beacon Hill area. This caller was near the intersection of East Francis Avenue and North Freya Street, approximately 1.3 miles northwest of the fire. The caller described a dark smoke plume that was "not very large."

At approximately 2:50 PM, Jeremy, a staff member at Beacon Hill Catering & Events Center (BHCE) on East Valley Springs Road, spotted smoke in the trees about 1/4 mile north of the Center. He informed other staff members. One of them called 911.

About five minutes earlier than these first 911 calls, Tyler Reisdorph, a firefighter on DNR Engine 440, spotted a small puff of white smoke in the timber just west of the Bonneville power lines that cross Little Mount Baldy.

Engine 440 had been heading north on Market Street. They were paired up with Kitsap Brush 85 and patrolling the area. In an attempt to "get eyes on" the fire, Engine 440 and Brush 85 continued north on Market Street and turned east onto East Wellesley Avenue. East Wellesley transitions into East Valley Springs Road.

Engine Boss Jason Beck estimated the two engines arrived on the scene three to five minutes after having first observed the smoke. Upon their arrival at 2:50 PM, Beck reported the fire to the Northeast Washington Interagency Coordinating Center (NEWICC), stating, "It's putting up a good column of smoke."

The fire was about mid-slope on a western exposure known as Little Mount Baldy. Jason sent crew members Brady and Kris, to hike up the powerline access road to size up the fire. Their hike was about 250 yards upslope, putting them about 150 feet higher than Valley Springs Road.

When they arrived at the fire, they estimated it was 1/2 acre in size on a western exposure in grass, brush, and Ponderosa Pine. It was creeping and backing west, against the wind and downslope, but running hard to the northeast, pushed by a 20-plus mph southwest wind. Several small spot fires had already formed just ahead of the fire. The spot fires were along the power line access corridor, a treeless 300-foot-wide corridor that protects the powerlines from contacting the 30- to 60-foot-tall Ponderosa Pines that cover the surrounding hillsides. Flame heights were two to six feet, and the fire front was about 30 feet wide, running laterally on the hill to the east and upslope to the northeast.

After sizing up the fire, Brady and Kris hustled down the hill to Engine 440. At 2:55 PM, the fire began spotting across the powerline corridor into heavy timber.

Jason radioed DNR's Dispatch and asked, "Do we have a FireBoss or other air resources?"

Dispatch replied, "Nothing at Deer Park. What are your resources at risk?"

"We have structures threatened; one structure is about 100 yards from the fire," he replied.

Dispatch told him there were two Fire Bosses in Coeur D'Alene. A Fire Boss is a single-seat amphibious aircraft that carries 500 gallons of water or retardant. The agility, tempo, and effectiveness of the Fire Boss exceed all other air resources.

Jason replied, "I want Fire Bosses, the AA, and the rotor. The hazards are the powerlines overhead. The fire is two to three acres, running and torching."

By asking for the AA and the rotor, Jason requested a designated Air Attack Supervisor and a fire attack helicopter carrying a 500-gallon bucket for dropping water on the fire. From these early communications, Jason correctly recognized that the fire had a significant potential to grow and spread. It was a major risk to the surrounding area.

According to the DNR Fire Investigation Report, in the early stages of the fire, numerous posts appeared on social media about the fire. Most contained pictures showing gray and black smoke leaning over in the wind at a 45-degree angle. When Jason asked for those two Fire Bosses, the Wellesley Fire was off and running. The two brush trucks already on the scene would never be able to catch it.

As described earlier, Spokane County Dispatch received three separate 911 calls—the first two described only a vague general location for the fire. The third 911 call from BHCE was used to establish a specific address for the fire. However, the address used was the calling party's address, not the fire's location, which resulted in Spokane County Dispatch sending the wrong people to the fire.

The Spokane City Fire Department's (SFD) jurisdiction coverers the location of the BHCE and everything *south* of East Valley Springs Road. SCFD9's jurisdiction covers everything north of East Valley Springs Road. The fire was in SCFD9, not the city of Spokane. Did this make a difference? I think it might have.

In 2016, SFD had no brush trucks or water tenders. As an urban fire department, they had limited resources for, and experience of, fighting wildfires in red flag conditions. Did that matter? Consider this. The most critical skill set during scene size-up and initial attack (IA) on a fire like the Wellesley Fire was the ability to recognize what would happen in the next 60 minutes, know what resources were needed instantly, and know how they should be deployed. Unfortunately, in 2016, the typical frontline urban firefighters in SFD didn't have these skills because most of their crews didn't have years of experience fighting large wildland fires in extreme weather conditions.

As good as SFD is on urban fires, the Wellesley Fire was different. In contrast, SCFD9 is a rural fire district with many command personnel and frontline firefighters with extensive wildland experience. SCFD9 also has brush trucks and water tenders for fighting wildland fires. So, from the start, the Wellesley Fire had a head start on the folks best suited to stop it.

Fortunately, some initial responses from the closest SCDF9 resources started even though they were not dispatched. This happened because Stations 94 and 92 crews monitored the early radio traffic from SFD's responding units. Because the radio traffic indicated the location of the fire was in SCFD9, not SFD, both B92 and E94 immediately headed for the fire.

At about the same time, SCFD9's Chief, Jack Cates, became aware of the fire. He immediately responded code to the fire and radioed Spokane County Dispatch, telling them the fire was in District 9, not SFD. He ordered an extreme wildland response from District 9 and reported, "We have spot fires from Valley Springs all the way to the top of Baldy." It was 3:01 PM, about 30 minutes after the start of the fire and 10 minutes after DNR engine 440 had arrived on the scene.

SCFD9's Assistant Chief, Doug Bleeker, who was now arriving on the fire scene, radioed Dispatch, "We've got half-mile to one-mile spotting upslope ahead of the fire, with ground runs and group torching."

Less than six minutes later, at 3:07 PM, Jason Beck, on Engine 440, updated DNR Dispatch of the fire's progress, "The fire has crossed the powerline right-of-way and is into the timber."

At 3:19, Unified Command had been established, meaning that Chief Cates and Jason Beck were now working together. They called DNR Dispatch asking for more air support, stating, "If we have any heavies, we need to get them headed this way."

The request for "heavies" refers to large air tankers carrying thousands of gallons of fire retardants. Command was now looking into the future and could see that the earlier request for two Fire Bosses and one rotor was inadequate to stop the fire.

Dispatch replied, "We need to know resources at risk for prioritizing aircraft."

Command replied, "Multiple structures and large propane tanks."

Dispatch responded, "We need to know if these are primary residences or secondary structures, as we have four fires asking for aircraft, and we are trying to prioritize accordingly."

This message from Dispatch let everyone know there were several other large active fires in the area, and incident commanders on those fires were all asking for air support. To use what was available efficiently and effectively, decisions would have to be made.

Command replied, "We are seeing multiple primary residences threatened, and the fire is close to town."

At 3:30 PM, Command updated DNR Dispatch, "We are estimating the fire is 50 to 60 acres and making solid runs with torching. Do we have tail numbers for the incoming aircraft?"

Dispatch replied, "We have diverted heavies to your incident. We will get back with details."

At 3:40 PM, Command contacted DNR dispatch with another update, "I haven't heard from Air Attack over the scene yet. Right now, the fire is 80 to 100 acres, with very active behavior, torching and running. The county (Sheriff) is in the process of doing evacuations east of the fire. Fire is still pushing to the northeast …"

I'm sure Command felt a little better knowing the heavies were coming, but the fire was growing, and now it was threatening dozens of homes. Luckily, because the heavy aircraft were being diverted from other local fires rather than parked on the ground somewhere, they arrived just minutes later at 3:44 PM.

It was 3:54 PM when Command gave their next update, "We are getting more resources arriving on the incident. Air resources are trying to make drops along both flanks. Report from Air Attack is that the fire has spotted over Bigelow Gulch Road."

At the same time as this last report, Gary, Matt, and I were on our way to the fire in B96. But, before I get to that, let me go back in time and describe some specifics about what had been happening with two crews from SCFD9 that had already arrived on the scene.

When Chief Cates arrived on the fire at about 3:00 PM, he established Unified Command with DNR. He then began assigning the arriving resources to structure protection in the areas most threatened by the rapidly advancing fire. Given the terrain, wind, and the head start the fire had, he knew that chasing the fire was futile. He had to get resources out ahead of it.

Chief Cates was experienced enough to know getting crews in the path of a fire like this was dangerous. But he also knew his crews were well trained, experienced, and would make good decisions. They would know when to stay and fight and when to retreat. Consequently, when B92 arrived, Chief Cates sent them east on Valley Springs Road to prep defensible residences.

The engine boss on B92 was Lieutenant Cody Traber. Cody had years of wildland training and experience and used it to maximum effect. He and his crew saved several homes that day, some by pushing the fire around them and one by lighting a backfire to burn out the fuels surrounding the house just before the fire arrived. In another instance, when they were about to get overrun, they made the right call to retreat down to Valley Springs Road, move east, and continue their assignment. Their experience helped them to act effectively, independently, and safely.

Farther east and higher on the flank of Little Baldy, E94 was the next arriving SCFD9 unit. At one point, they were confronted with 50-plus mph wind gusts. The structures they were attempting to protect were high-end homes at the uppermost point of a residential development extending up Baldy's east flank. There was very little timber in and around this part of the development, but the three-foot high dry grass surrounding the homes was putting up 6-to-10-foot flames and burning like paper. When the fast-moving firefront reached these upper-level homes, only those with significant defensive areas were savable.

In the early stages of the fire, I was at home listening to my radio scanner when the original calls to SFD resources went out. The fire alarm also came out on Pulse Point, a free smartphone application that posts fire department alarms. I texted our Station 96 text chain about the fire because I anticipated we would get called to fight it. When Chief Cates began asking for SCFD9 resources, I headed to Station 96 to get ready. Gary, Matt, and Mark did the same. A short time later, Captain Don's wife, Renee, told him, "Don, you should come see this." She was referring to the large column of smoke growing on the eastern horizon. He took one look and headed for the station.

The origin of the fire was about seven miles southwest of Station 96. Soon, we were all dressed in our PPE and standing outside the station, watching the column grow and smelling the smoke. We also listened to our radios, waiting for the call to respond. Based on what we were hearing, we all wondered why we had not already been dispatched. About 30 minutes after the first units arrived on the scene, Chief Cates requested strike teams of additional structural engines and brush trucks from surrounding districts, but our pagers were silent. We hesitated to add ourselves to the fire because units were expected to remain in their stations until called. We wondered if we had not been called because we were needed at the district's east end to respond to additional fires. We were wrong.

Minutes later, we heard Chief Cates asking for an update on all responding units. After Dispatch gave him a rundown of the growing list, he asked, "Have you toned Brush 96?"

"Negative," responded Dispatch.

Cates replied, "Add them to the call."

Matt, Gary, and I jumped in B96 and headed out before our pagers went off. Matt was driving, I was in the officer's seat, and Gary was squeezed between us. I seldom get nervous heading to brush fires. This one was different. We were all nervous.

Don stayed at the station with Mark and contacted Assistant Chief Jim Walkowski, who had taken the role of the 921 Officer. Chief Walkowski's assignment as 921 was to manage all the district's resources. Jim told Don that two volunteers were standing by at Station 94 and would be instructed to report to Station 96. Once at Station 96, the Station 94 volunteers' assignment was to take WT96 and stage it at Station 94 (about a mile east of the fire). Don and Mark were assigned to pick them up in E96 and respond to the fire. When they arrived at the fire, they were immediately assigned structure protection on East Lyons Road, which was very near the head of the fire.

In the meantime, Matt, Gary, and I were headed west on Bigelow Gulch Road towards the growing smoke column. We could see the dark gray column leaning to the northeast. Several Fire Bosses and a tanker had passed overhead, making water and retardant drops.

About a mile from the fire, we heard Unified Command update DNR's Dispatch that air support believed the fire had jumped East Bigelow Gulch Road. It was 3:54 PM. We were driving west on Bigelow and immediately searched the horizon north of Bigelow. We saw no evidence of smoke. We were hoping air support was mistaken because just North of Bigelow are hundreds of homes surrounded by timber and agricultural fields. Many homes would have been lost if the fire had, in fact, jumped Bigelow.

It was 3:57 PM when we heard Unified Command contact Dispatch, "We're getting lots of active spotting and torching. We have reports of spots over Theirman Road into the Lyons Road area…."

We were approaching Theirman Road when we heard of the spotfires. The fire had indeed jumped Theirman Road (east of the fire) and was potentially headed toward the community of Northwoods, a dense residential development.

When we arrived at Theirman Road, we ran into a massive traffic jam of onlookers. Theirman Road borders the east perimeter of the Little Mt. Baldy area. It was our access to the fire and the place where we were most needed. Yet, even with lights and sirens, we were stranded in a sea of slow-moving cars and pedestrians. Countless onlookers had parked their cars on both sides of the road and were standing in the road taking video and pictures of the fire. Not only were they impeding our access, but they were also impeding residents trying to evacuate the area.

Moving forward at about three mph, we eventually got clear of the traffic jam at a point where a Sheriff had closed the road. Just then, a DNR "overhead" (DNR's term for command-level personnel) waved us down and walked briskly up to my window.

"Brush 96, I want you to turn left up that driveway and attack the fire that has jumped Theirman. Protect the house and chase down any additional spotfires. You are now in Division Yankee, I'm Arcadia 31, and Yankee Command. We are on DNR Tac 2."

"Copy that, Yankee Division, Tac 2," I replied.

I told Matt to go halfway up the driveway, park and hit the fire all along the fence line. I radioed Chief Cates and told him where we were and the nature of our assignment.

"Thanks, good, that was the plan," he replied.

We bailed out of the truck, Matt fired up the pump, and we started knocking down the fire that had spread about 150 yards up the driveway. The grass was short, so the flame lengths were only a foot or two. We made quick progress putting out the fire and extinguishing split-rail fence posts as we made our way to the house. Once at the house, we cut open a section of fence between two posts so Matt could drive the truck into what looked like four acres or more of the burning horse corral and grass. We knocked down all the spot fires that had spread throughout the corral and then put out the fire on the south perimeter of the property.

At 4:08 PM, while we were working the fire on Theirman, Unified Command updated Dispatch, "Air resources are trying to work the flanks and pinch off the head of the fire. Crews are trying to work on the spot east of Theirman. Currently, I have no number of the structures lost. There's lots of black smoke. Currently, county resources are working on closing Bigelow Gulch Road and any roads near the fire."

While working the corral, we saw a large residence about 100 yards away on the west side of Theirman catch fire. Engine 98 had been assigned structural protection for the house, but the yard was filled with brush and trees that torched when the ground fire passed. There was nothing the fire crew could do to stop the burning trees from igniting the back deck and roof of the house. The crew were spraying water on the house when Assistant Chief Jeffries commanded them over the radio, "Do not engage the house fire. I repeat, do not engage the house fire."

It was hard to watch, but it was the right call. There's no way a crew of three or four firefighters in wildland gear can effectively attack a burning residence. It just puts them at additional extreme risk. Whenever a structure is surrounded by fuels and catches fire, it must be abandoned. Whoever lived in that house would lose everything in the next 30 minutes.

At 5:03 PM, Unified Command's update to Dispatch was, "Still guessing 150 to 200 acres. We're trying to get the fire stopped at Theirman Road. The smoke column is lying down to the northeast, so we have lots of smoke. I can't see if we've gotten more spots than the one confirmed spot past Theirman."

We were the "crews" working on the spot fire referred to by Unified Command, and the house fire we were witnessing was at least some of the black smoke he was seeing.

Within the hour, the fire front had passed our position, and the winds decreased, which lessened the threat of the fire jumping Theirman Road again in additional locations. Radio traffic indicated a second residence had been lost up high in the development, and a dozen or so outbuildings had burned.

Air attack was in full force overhead, and you could feel the vibrations created by the sound of the jet engines as the planes roared overhead just feet above the trees. A pair of heavy tankers were now pounding the leading edges of the fire to the south, east, and north with their red slurry of fire retardant. With their turboprop engines screaming just over the treetops, the two Fire Bosses repeatedly dropped their 500-gallon loads of water on hot spots in the center of the fire. It was the most significant air show I had ever seen while on a fire. Being this close was exciting and unnerving. We have all seen the terrible videos of fire attack aircraft losing a wing and slamming into the ground in an explosion of fire. We didn't want to see anything like that again, never mind having it happen right before our eyes on a fire.

As the sun started to set, the temperature and wind dropped, and the humidity started to rise, which all helped diminish the fire activity. Hand crews and dozer crews were starting to make headway encircling the fire. The decreased intensity of the fire also allowed a few crews to hit hotspots inside the perimeter.

Unified Command's update to Dispatch at 5:54 PM was," We are making good progress on the right flank, and the dozer is getting an anchor point on the left. Aircraft have done good work on boxing in the fire and are trying to cut across the head and pinch it off."

Forward progress of the fire was now being slowed dramatically. As the afternoon progressed into early evening, we learned the fire would transition to a State Mobilization, meaning statewide resources would take over management of the fire sometime later that night. The Division Supervisors were now looking for crews willing to spend the night working the fire. Gary and I decided that the night work was better left to guys who weren't as "gray of beard and long of tooth" as we. Matt was game to stay, but we outvoted him.

Sometime around 9 PM, we were released from the fire. We had been working about five hours straight, but it went quickly. My back and feet were aching, and we were all hungry and filthy, so it felt good to head home. It was another 24 hours before crews fully established a line around the fire, and not until Tuesday or Wednesday that residents were allowed to return to their homes.

I've only touched on the actions of a few District 9 crews in this story because these were the ones I was aware of and remembered. But I would be remiss not to mention that dozens of crews from Spokane County fought the Wellesley fire. Over 220 career and volunteer firefighters from DNR, SCFD9, SFD, District 4, District 8, Spokane Valley Fire, and other agencies played essential roles in stopping the fire. Over 20 fire engine companies and five water tenders worked on the fire that first day. They certainly all deserve mention. I'll bet they all have stories to tell.

Several days after the fire, Chief Cates held an after-action discussion for all District 9 units that worked the fire. He started the meeting by showing us a recording of his dashcam video as he drove to the fire. Seeing the early stages of the fire's growth as he approached from the northwest was impressive. The video also contained the audio from his radio. It was amazing how calm most of the incoming units' communications were.

Chief Cates then asked each crew boss to identify their unit and describe their role on the fire. When it was my turn, I described our work on Theirman Road. The Chief stated that B96 prevented the fire from burning down the

Northwoods development. It was a bit of an overstatement of the facts, but it felt good, nonetheless, for our efforts to be appreciated.

After hearing the stories from B92 and E94, the entire group was impressed with their accomplishments. The Chief said he'd never been prouder of District 9 crews on a fire, and his voice cracked a bit with emotion when speaking of it. It was a fire he described as a career fire for District 9. I didn't say anything, but I couldn't help thinking that for Station 96, career fires seem to be adding up.

On our way back to the station after the meeting, we discussed how it would be even harder to fight a fire like the Wellesley Fire on Forker Ridge. Most of Forker Ridge is much steeper than Little Mt. Baldy, and many roads are one way in and one way out. Protecting homes on the ridge would be a risky assignment none of us wanted to consider. But we will think about it. We'll think about it every time we go to bed, knowing red flag warnings are posted for the next day. It's when, not if, it will happen. It's just a matter of time.

Chapter 19

Gary, Don't Go in There!

This story is about two EMS calls during the winter of 2012. Over the years, Station 96 has responded to an address on East Farwell several times for both EMS calls and a structure fire. The house is a 1,000-square-foot home built in the mid-seventies on a 10-acre parcel of timbered land. It's just over a mile north of Station 96. The homeowners were elderly, and the family was well-known by most folks in the community.

In this part of East Farwell, the gravel road drops steeply down to North Forker Road from its intersection with North Peck Road. It's downhill, about a 15% grade, and barely wide enough for two cars traveling in opposite directions. There are only two homes on this stretch of Farwell.

My first call to this address was a 31D for difficulty breathing. The patient was an elderly male with a history of COPD. It was about 9 PM when the call came in. I was the first to arrive at the station, and I pulled the truck out on the ramp to wait for an additional crew member. When Gary arrived, he climbed into the officer's seat, and we headed out.

It had been snowing all day, with about 6-8 inches of snow on the road. Neither North Peck nor East Farwell had been plowed, so we were glad we had taken the time earlier in the day to chain up B96. I slipped it into four-wheel drive as we left the bay.

Both E94 and an AMR ambulance were also responding, but because of the heavy snow, we knew they would be driving slowly and anticipated being on the scene for a long time by ourselves. Gary and I are EMTs and can handle most medical and trauma situations, but it's always comforting to have a paramedic just a few minutes behind us.

The ninety-degree right turn from Peck onto Farwell slopes away a bit, so as I made the turn, the front end of the truck refused to grip, and we slid halfway across the road before getting enough traction to make the turn.

Anticipating the steep descent to the residence, I turned to Gary and said sarcastically, "Oh, this is gonna be fun."

"Yeah. I hope E94 and the AMR are chained up," he replied.

The house was 200 yards down the hill. I slowly drove down Farwell, looking for the driveway. There were no streetlights on Farwell, so it was dark except for our headlights reflecting off the falling snow. When we finally got to the driveway, we could see that it angled off the road, so there was a good chance we could make the turn, which we did. Once in the front yard, I did a three-point turn to reposition the truck facing out of the driveway while still leaving room for the ambulance. We climbed out, grabbed our gear, and headed up the stairs to the front door.

Olivia met us at the door. Her husband was the patient, who was in the master bedroom. He was feeling ill and having difficulty breathing even though he was on a nose cannula getting 100% oxygen at about three liters per minute. We went through the usual routine of getting vitals and a medical history. Except for a low blood oxygen saturation, his vitals were stable. But he was very uncomfortable and wanted to go to the hospital. Olivia also wanted him to go.

Just about then, E94 called us on the radio. Instead of approaching Farwell from North Peck as we had, they had taken North Forker Road and were now parked at the bottom of East Farwell, about 600 yards east of our location. Lieutenant Oliver, the officer and paramedic on E94, looked up into the pitch black at a narrow, snow-filled road that climbed steeply through the timber. He was sure they'd never make it up the hill in their engine. The AMR unit was parked behind them, and concluded they'd not be able to make it to the house either.

Gary gave Oliver a patient update, and Oliver agreed the patient should be transported. But he told Gary we'd have to bring the patient down the hill in B96. Gary asked Oliver to stand by.

Gary explained all this to the couple, and they agreed to give it a try. The plan was to get the patient dressed in warm clothes, walk him outside, and get him into the brush truck. The brush truck we had back then only had a single front bench seat, so it would have to be just me and the patient going down the hill. It took a while, but we eventually got him in the truck without any issues. I climbed in, radioed Oliver we were on our way down and started to pull out of the driveway.

The driveway approached Farwell at an angle that put us pointing west up the hill, not east down the hill. Because there was no way to turn around in the deep snow without sliding out of control down the hill, or worse, off the road into the trees, I decided to pull out onto Farwell facing west and then back down the hill to the waiting ambulance.

It was a slow drive backward down the hill, using only my mirrors to peer into the dark. Eventually, I began to see the flashing glow of the emergency lights on E94 in my mirrors. A few more yards and we had made it.

At the bottom of the hill, we loaded the patient into the ambulance. My job was done. With relief, I headed back up to get Gary and our gear. Thirty minutes later, we were back at the station. While driving home, I wondered out loud, "What would have happened if you and I hadn't shown up?" "We'll never know," said Gary.

Several months later, we again received a page for a 31D at the same Farwell address. It was early spring, so we didn't have to worry about snow this time. It was close to midnight. I was in bed, in deep sleep, when my pager woke me up. The ride to the station seemed long and difficult because I was only half awake. When I got there, I checked my phone for texts. Only Gray was headed to the station.

On the drive north along Peck Road, Dispatch gave us the short. We had a 70-year-old male with stage four lung cancer. He was conscious but not responsive. Both E94 and an AMR unit were also responding.

When we arrived on the scene, everything looked a bit familiar. However, the surrounding area was now pitch black and haunting without all the white reflective snow we had last time. Time and weather had not been kind to the house and its outbuildings. They all showed their age, having been built in the 1970s, and were surrounded by heavy overhanging trees and thick brush.

We parked in the driveway, leaving room for AMR, climbed out of the truck, gathered our gear, and headed for the long flight of wooden steps leading up to the front door. Halfway to the stairs, I asked Gary,

"Do you have the radio?"

"No, I thought you had it," he said.

"Go ahead up; I'll get it," I replied and headed back to the truck.

Dispatch called for us on the mobile radio as I opened the truck door.

"Brush 96, Dispatch," she called.

I grabbed the mic from the dash.

"Dispatch, go for Brush 96."

"Bruch 96, we just had a call from the residence that a man was trying to get into the residence to steal drugs from the patient. They believe he is armed."

"Brush 96 Copy."

"Oh, shit," I thought as I dropped the mic and ran to the bottom of the stairs to stop Gary from entering the house. Looking up, I could see Gary's dark silhouette standing at the top of the stairs on the small landing. He was knocking on the door.

I yelled to him in a forced whisper from the bottom of the stairs,

"Gary, don't go in there!"

Gary slowly turned and looked down at me. "What?"

"Don't go in there! Dispatch said a guy with a weapon might be in the house," I whisper-yelled.

Suddenly, the door jerked open, startling Gary and making him step back abruptly. A woman was standing in the doorway. Gary stepped back again as much as the landing allowed to get some space between himself and the woman.

"Who are you?" she asked.

"The Fire Department," Gary said, more than a bit startled.

I yelled to the woman from the bottom of the stairs, "Does anyone in the house have a weapon?"

"What?"

"Does anyone in the house have a weapon?"

There was a pause. "No, why?" she replied, surprised by the question.

"Are you sure no one in the house has a weapon?" I said as calmly as I could but with authority.

"Yeah," she said with a small but reassuring degree of conviction.

I explained, "They told us on the radio someone in the house called 911 and said there was a man with a weapon trying to steal drugs."

She was quiet for a few seconds, which caused my heart to skip a beat, and said, "Oh, that was me. I called 911 because Olivia's grandson was here earlier trying to steal some of his grandpa's drugs. He also took his grandpa's gun when he left. We thought the knocking on the door was him trying to get back in."

I was halfway up the stairs and unsure what to do. Gary picked up our BLS bag and slowly followed her into the house. My heart was still racing as

I carefully climbed the remaining stairs. While I walked through the house towards the bedroom, I snuck a peek into each room as I passed them to be sure no one else was in the house. I was spooked for sure.

The young woman who had answered the door was a hired caregiver. As I entered the bedroom, she explained to Gary that the patient was not alert most of the day and had been diagnosed with stage four lung cancer. Our patient was the man I had driven down the hill in the snow a few months ago. He had deteriorated significantly and had been diagnosed with lung cancer in addition to COPD.

Olivia was also in the bedroom. She was understandably very concerned about her husband. When I asked her what had changed in his condition this past week that caused her to call us tonight, she told us his condition seemed worse, and the caregiver suggested she call 911. We could hear the crew from E94 climbing the front steps, so we asked the caregiver to go and let them in the house.

The patient was conscious but not alert. He was getting 100% oxygen via a nose cannula, but his oxygen saturation was in the low 90s. His heart rate was high, and his blood pressure was low. He appeared to be dehydrated.

Lieutenant Oliver, the officer and paramedic on E94, walked into the room. He had been one of the first paramedics hired by SCFD9 in the 1980s, and we had often worked with him. We gave him a patient update, and he asked if the patient had an Advanced Directive for Care. The caregiver and Olivia thought he did, but after a brief search of the house, they came up empty.

This is a situation we sometimes run into. The patient is very ill, and there's no Advanced Directive to indicate what we can or cannot do. Oliver explained to Olivia that the best course of action was to transport her husband to the hospital, but it would have to be *her* decision. This is where things stalled.

Olivia was becoming very emotional and started repeatedly saying more to herself than us, that she wasn't sure what to do. She was standing in this small bedroom with five firefighters and two ambulance personnel, and her husband was lying in bed, close to death. Everyone was looking at her, waiting for her decision. It was all just too much, and she froze.

Perhaps she often relied on her husband for important decisions. Or maybe she was afraid he'd never return home if he went to the hospital. It became very difficult to watch her struggle with the situation.

Many years ago, I sat in a hospital room all night and watched my father die of lung cancer. He died in an unfamiliar hospital bed in an unfamiliar room. It was a horrible thing to watch and impossible to forget. Perhaps, instinctively, she feared something similar was about to happen. Maybe she was praying silently for guidance. I don't know.

It was getting very late, perhaps close to 1 AM, and Oliver pressed her to decide. But she couldn't do it. He decided to search once again for the Advanced Directive. At the time, it seemed that Lieutenant Oliver needed to leave the room to ease his building frustration.

As Oliver searched the kitchen, Gary and I tried calming and reassuring Olivia. We told her it was tough to know what to do, but perhaps her husband would be more comfortable in the hospital. They could give him fluids and pain meds, and maybe he'd be able to get a good night's rest. She thought about it for about a minute and decided, yes, taking him to the hospital was probably best.

When Oliver returned without finding the Advanced Directive, we told him Olivia had decided to have her husband transported to the hospital. "OK, let's go," he said.

The patient was transferred to the ambulance gurney within minutes and headed out the door. Gary and I stayed with Olivia and helped her gather her things so she could follow the ambulance in her car. She was still a bit unsure, and she became agitated with herself when she couldn't find her phone and purse. We helped her find the phone and purse, and she settled down.

Eventually, Gary and I found ourselves driving back to the station. We were both tired and a bit sad about the whole thing. For us, watching Olivia try to deal with the imminent death of her husband was a struggle. We were strangers to Olivia before that first snowy night's call months ago. But now, we'd remember her for years to come. We would see Olivia one more time a few months later.

It was late June when we saw her again and learned that Olivia's husband had died soon after going to the hospital. The annual Foothill Community picnic occurs in the community center's parking lot, just across the street from Station 96. Most of the volunteers attend, and we stage the fire trucks on the ramp where the attendees can come by and see them. It gives everyone in the neighborhood a chance to see how some of their property taxes are spent and allows the local kids to climb all over the trucks.

Unexpectedly, during the picnic, Olivia came to the station to thank us for helping her through that difficult night. It was bittersweet to receive her thanks, and it almost brought me to tears. Her words meant a lot to both Gary and me. To this day, Olivia's kind words of thanks have made it easier for me to get out of bed in the middle of the night when the pager goes off. I'm sure Gary feels the same way.

Chapter 20

Hey, I Don't Have a Pulse Guys!

On most of our EMS calls, we make our initial patient contact as soon as possible. Those first few minutes with the patient usually give us a very accurate sense of the type and severity of the emergency. However, I have learned from experience that a patient's condition can change quickly. And when it changes quickly, it is seldom a good thing.

It was a Friday in mid-March when we received a 31D call. The address was about three and 1/2 miles north of Station 96. After a brisk ride through the woods in my RZR, I saw Captain Don's truck parked outside the station, so I knew he was waiting for me in B96. When I climbed in the driver's seat, Don said, "North on Forker, about a half mile past Scribner on the left."

Because of the location, I knew E92 would be coming from north of the address, and we would probably beat them to the scene. Don let Dispatch know over the radio we were responding. As we drove past Scribner Road, Gary was waiting in his car at the intersection and followed us to the scene.

The dispatcher gave us the short, "You have a 50-year-old female who fell. She's conscious and alert but cannot get up. Her husband is with her. She was returning from the hospital after hip replacement surgery. Enter through the garage."

The gravel driveway was long and rose steeply uphill just before getting to the house. A two-car garage was behind the house, so we pulled up in front of it. One of the garage doors was open, with a car parked in front of the open door. We climbed out, put on our masks and gloves, grabbed the EMS bag and AED, and walked towards the garage.

As I approached the car, a man walked out of the garage and met me.

"She's in the garage by the door," he said and pointed towards the person door in the back corner of the garage.

"Is she conscious?" I asked, walking with him towards the front of the car.

"Yes, but she can't get up. We just got back from the hospital. She had a hip replacement. She was walking into the house when she got dizzy and fell."

"Did she lose consciousness," I asked.

"I don't think so," he said.

"What's her name? You're her husband?"

"It's Jackie. Yeah, she's my wife."

"And what's your name?" I asked as I approached her and set down my EMS bag and AED.

"Bill"

I knelt down next to Jackie and did my best to speak slowly and calmly.

"Hi Jackie, I'm with the Fire Department. I understand you got dizzy and fell, is that right?"

"Yes," she replied softly, looking up at me.

"Do you have any pain?" I asked.

"No," she said as she shook her head a bit left and right.

"Jackie, try to keep your head still when you answer, OK?"

"Do you think you hit your head when you fell?" I asked.

"No, I don't think so," she said again softly.

"Did you hurt your hip when you fell?"

"No."

"Are you still dizzy?"

"Yes."

"Did you trip or fall from being dizzy?"

"Dizzy, I think."

"Is it OK if I take your blood pressure and measure your heart rate?"

She nodded yes.

I was relieved she was conscious and alert, but the fact that she had not tried to get up worried me.

By now, E92 had pulled up, and Don directed their medic to me. I didn't recognize the medic, but people sometimes trade shifts, so it was not unusual. He stood back, looked down at me and Jackie and said, "What do you have?"

"This is Jackie. She just came home from the hospital after having hip surgery. When she walked into the garage, she got dizzy and fell. She has no pain but is still dizzy. That's all I've got so far," I said.

"OK," the medic said as he turned to the crew behind him. "Let's get some vitals and an ECG and move her out to the middle of the garage."

When I returned my gaze to Jackie, she looked at me and said, "I can't breathe." Then, her eyes closed.

"Jackie, Jackie," I said loudly. No response.

"Jackie, Jackie, can you hear me?" I said a bit louder. No response.

I checked her carotid pulse. Nothing.

"Guys, I don't have a pulse," I said. No one seemed to hear me.

"Hey guys, I do not have a pulse!" I said more deliberately and much louder. The AMR crew was rolling a gurney into the garage. Just as I was about to start CPR, the medic said, "Let's get her on the gurney."

The crew rushed over. Gary was standing next to me, and we picked her up and put her on the ambulance gurney so they could move her into the center of the garage and have more room to work. I stepped back as the E92 medic had taken over patient care.

I took a few steps around the gurney to Pat, the officer on E92.

"How about the helo?" I said in his ear.

"Yeah, good idea," he said without looking at me as he was focusing on the crew working on Jackie.

I turned to Don, who was standing next to Pat.

"Pat wants the helo," I said.

Don grabbed the mic on his portable and walked out of the garage to call Dispatch.

"Dispatch, this is Brush 96."

"Go ahead, Brush 96."

"Dispatch, launch Life Flight."

"Copy, launching Life Flight."

Don, Gary, and I walked around to the front of the house and looked down the driveway to find a landing zone for the helo. Gary pointed out two possible areas. While Don headed down to inspect them, Gary headed back into the garage to help with CPR. I jogged over to B96, turned it around, and drove it down the long driveway to block any traffic that might come up the driveway.

We selected the LZ and then set out a circle of emergency cones so the pilot could easily see the area. At the same time, Rob, our District Training Officer, pulled into the entrance of the driveway in his pickup and parked. He called Dispatch and told them he would be the ground contact for Life Flight and would be on radio channel 4-dash-8. All we had to do was wait for the bird.

Up in the garage, the crews were working on the patient. Initially, they had started CPR on the gurney. But, when Gary returned to the garage, Pat told him to grab a backboard from E94 and put it under the patient. Once that was done, they loaded the gurney in the ambulance while continuing CPR and drove down to the LZ.

Life Flight landed soon after the AMR unit arrived at the LZ. Over the next five minutes, the ambulance crew established ROSC, which means that Jackie's heart was now pumping on its own. They loaded her in the helicopter, and the bird was soon in the air and disappearing over the ridge. As the sound of the rotors and jet engine faded, it became very quiet, and time seemed to stop.

The noise of a helicopter always dominates the scene during one of these operations. As it arrives and approaches the LZ, all you hear is the rotor slap. That's the loud noise you hear and feel in your chest, sometimes described as a chop, chop (thus, the slang term "chopper") and emphasized as the audio signature of helicopters in most war movies. But, when the pilot commits to landing, the jet engine's whine and the rotors' powerful downwash are all you hear and feel. Once on the ground, the pilot idles down the jet, and the rotors spin relatively slowly and silently, and then the area becomes washed in the steady, high-pitched whine of the jet and the smell of jet exhaust. Once the patient is loaded, the whine of the jet multiplies tenfold, and the rotor wash assaults you, often slinging gravel and small sticks, culminating with a big blast of rotor downwash as the pilot lifts off and slowly rises above the trees and power lines. When the nose of the bird dips and accelerates away, the fading rotor slap signals the end of the operation. The radio sequence between ground contact and Dispatch makes it official.

"Dispatch, 930," Rob called.

"This is Dispatch. Go ahead 930."

"Life Flight is in the air."

"Copy, Life Flight is in the air," replied Dispatch.

The call was over. We had done everything we could. All we could do now was hope things turned out well for Jackie and her husband. I wasn't optimistic.

Over the past 26 years, I've been on hundreds of EMS calls, but none were like this one. Most of the calls have followed a pattern. We get the call for a particular problem, such as a cardiac emergency, difficulty breathing, a broken leg, a possible broken hip, a burn, or a seizure. In each instance, we quickly uncover the central issue and provide a short-term solution before shipping the patient to the hospital. That's our role in the emergency medicine paradigm: get there first, mitigate life threats, package, and initiate patient transport to a facility that can resolve the issue. There's a sense of certainty to it. Even if one of our patients were to die, we usually knew it was a possible outcome. But, on this call, when Life Flight disappeared over the ridge, and the sound of their rotors faded away, I had no idea what had happened to Jackie. The only thing I knew was that I was talking to her one minute, and a minute later, I was convinced I was the last person ever to hear her voice. As I drove B96 back to the station, I couldn't get that one thought out of my mind.

Over the years, I've learned that sometimes first responders need to know what happened to a patient after they disappeared down the road in an ambulance or over the ridge in a helicopter. We need to know if we correctly identified the problem. We need to know if we successfully employed an effective solution. We need to know if our efforts, the decisions we reached, and our work made a difference.

The day after this call, I learned that Jackie never regained consciousness. She died the following day. Although the cause of death was uncertain, the evidence indicated to the docs at the hospital that Jackie died of a pulmonary embolism. The embolism was probably a complication of her hip replacement surgery.

When I discovered what happened to Jackie, I didn't know what to make of it. I felt numb. I didn't know how to feel about it or learn from it. I didn't even know how to find value in it. I still don't.

In retrospect, what I do know is that, as first responders, we don't diagnose our patients. We treat signs and symptoms and do everything we can to protect the core, keep the patient alive, and give others the opportunity to diagnose and treat them. By doing these things successfully, we give others the opportunity to send them home to family and friends. It's what we do, and most of the time, it's enough. But not always.

<h1 style="text-align:center">Chapter 21</h1>

<h1 style="text-align:center">You Guys Wanna Save a House?</h1>

In the summer of 2022, we had a very slow wildland fire season. We only went to one significant wildland fire during the season, the Williams Lake Fire in Spokane County Fire District 3 (SCFD3). This chapter is about that one fire.

The 2022 fire season started with a cool, wet spring that wouldn't quit, lasting into the first four weeks of summer. Finally, in mid-July, a string of hot summer days arrived, making most folks forget what came before it. However, wildland firefighters don't forget wet springs. This is because they stimulate the growth of tons of grass and brush. Come August, the grass and brush are thoroughly dried, cured, and ready to burn.

Having lived in the inland northwest for 20 years, it was no surprise that our wet spring was immediately followed by 14 days of 90-plus-degree temperatures, with the last four days of that stretch averaging over 100 degrees. The first three days of August followed suit, resulting in a run of five out of eight days registering 100 degrees or higher. The frosting on the cake came on August 3rd when a Red Flag Warning went into effect for most of Eastern Washington for high temperatures, low humidity, and the expected arrival of high winds driven by a long-awaited cold front coming in from the southwest. Most folks looked forward to it. They were, understandably, tired of the oppressive heat wave. Wildland firefighters were more likely to think about the long, wet spring that created tons of fast burning grass and brush. And some of us were tired of going on mostly EMS calls and car accidents. We were ready to fight fire. It sounds crazy, but that's just the way it is.

It was early afternoon on Wednesday, August 3rd, when Larry, a local landowner, rode his John Deere tractor through one of his rocky fields on West Williams Lake Road. Because farming the rocky, dry land is next to impossible, the fields were full of tall, dry grass and brush. Much of the land in this part of Spokane County is called "Scablands." What are Scablands?

The Scablands of Eastern Washington got their name from early settlers who found it unsuitable for farming. The following abbreviated origin story of the Scablands is described on the Eastern Washington DNR website[3].

> During the last ice age, a lobe of ice at least a half-mile high blocked the Clark Fork River near the present-day Idaho and Montana border, creating an enormous natural reservoir – glacial lake Missoula. This ice dam failed – over and over – sending inconceivable volumes of water and ice rampaging across the land. The largest floods were equal to 10 times the modern flow of all the rivers of the world combined.

> Each thundering torrent of water, ice, and debris raced across the Rathdrum Prairie and into eastern Washington, stripping away tons of soil and rock and carving a region known as the Channeled Scabland.

While Larry was driving his tractor across these ancient rocky fields, he struck a rock with the undercarriage of a field mower he was towing. He later reported to the DNR Fire Investigator that he was not mowing at the time, but by striking a rock, he produced a spark big and hot enough to ignite the cured grass and brush filling the field. Larry recalled that he didn't notice any fire or smoke when he struck the rock. However, after driving his tractor into another field, he glanced back and saw fire spreading through the grass. The gusting winds, signaling the imminent arrival of the cold front, began to spread the fire alarmingly. There was nothing Larry could do except call 911.

It took eight days and nights to fully contain the Williams Lake Fire as it consumed 1,868 acres of scabland and timber. The official DNR Wildland Fire Investigation estimated the cost of fighting the fire was $3,115,100. Over 120 firefighting resources were used, 14 of which were aircraft. Fourteen agencies responded and fought the fire before it transitioned into a State Mobilization on August 4th. Although the advancing flames threatened 82 structures, only five were damaged or destroyed, none of which were primary residences. The progression of the fire was remarkable. Here's a timeline

3 https,//www.parks.wa.gov/225/Ice-Age-floods-in-Washington

of various estimates of the fire's size transmitted over the radio by various Incident Commanders as the fire grew.

The fire started as a tiny spark at 2:35 PM. At 2:48 PM, the fire was described as three to five acres. Ten minutes later, at 2:58 PM, it was estimated at five to seven acres. By 3:11 PM, it had grown to seven to ten acres. In another 14 minutes, it was estimated as 20 to 30 acres. This all means that in this early phase of the fire, it grew to 30 acres in just 50 minutes.

Here's the update by Incident Command at 3:57 PM, "Fire size is approximately 30 to 50 acres, it has spotted across Williams Lake Road and is still moving at a high rate of spread." Just 12 minutes later, at 4:09 PM, the estimate had grown to 75 acres. A few minutes later, Air Attack estimated the fire was 100 acres. By 4:35 PM, Incident Command requested a transition to a Type 3 State Mobilization Team later that evening. He also updated the fire's size to 100 to 150 acres. A couple of minutes later, Command confirmed the order for two VLATs (very large air tankers), two LATs (large air tankers), and a lead plane, which would control the air space above the fire. The fire had grown from a spark to perhaps 150 acres in just two hours, a spread rate of 75 acres per hour. Command's next update at 4:50 PM was, "Resources are engaged in point protection on the right flank. Approximately 20 to 30 structures are threatened."

The point protection he refers to means that engines are staged at specific residences to push the fire around them. Their focus on point protection resulted in only two structures being lost, both being outbuildings. But it also meant that the fire was spreading unabated.

At 5:32 PM, Air Attack estimated the fire had grown to 250 to 300 acres, stating that an actual size was difficult to estimate with the column of smoke laying over the fire. Level 3 evacuations had recently been put in place and were being implemented by the Spokane County Sheriff's Department. Over 100 structures, many of them residences, were threatened at one point.

By 6:35 PM, the fire had spotted over Rock Lake Road. The spot fire soon became a 40-acre fire that ran east to Long Road, which was lined with an additional dozen residences.

Here are a couple of quotes from a report by *The Spokesman Review* published on August 4th regarding the activity of the fire.[4]

---

4 https,//www.spokesman.com/stories/2022/aug/04/evacuation-orders-in-cheney-remain-fire-crews-main/

"Spokane County Fire District 3 Chief Cody Rohrbach said in a news conference Wednesday night the tall grasses, windy conditions, and rocky terrain have made it challenging to combat the blaze. In 28 years of fighting fire, I've never seen them like this, and so it's proved to be challenging for firefighters on the ground."

And this from a landowner on Williams Lake Road.

"As I pulled up, there were about 10 fire trucks in my driveway, up and down my property, and I couldn't even see my land," Warman said. "It was so smoky I could hardly breathe, and I couldn't even see 30 feet off the road to see if my house was on fire. Everything was engulfed in flames and smoke."

While all this was happening, Don, Matt, Jon, and I had been following the fire's progress by listening to the radio traffic on our radio scanners. We also had been exchanging texts about the fire and commenting on the long delay before SCFD3 could put resources on the fire. The first SCFD3 resource to arrive on the scene was one of their 320 Officers in a District SUV. This is what usually happens in District 3. Because volunteers staff most of the 11 fire stations, and only the duty officers are career firefighters, the duty officers get there first. The volunteers must drive to their stations, get into their PPE, and only then get their truck on the way. This situation exists because the fundamental challenge SCFD3 has is that it is the third largest fire district in Washington State, but it has a budget of less than five million dollars per year. Consequently, they have only 11 fire stations, predominantly staffed by volunteers.

Specifically, SCFD3 covers 570 square miles of rural land with many small communities. Because the population density is so low, the tax base is relatively small, and the budget is small. For comparison, SCFD3 is 4.6 times larger in square miles than SCDF9, yet SCFD3's budget is half that of the smaller but more populated SCFD9.

True to form, the first SCFD3 resource on the scene of the Willams Lake Fire was the 320 Duty Officer. When he arrived, he gave an excellent size-up and sounded relatively calm while waiting for resources that could put water on the fire. He initially sized up the fire at about 3 to 5 acres. Next on the scene, about one minute after 320, was their 322 Officer, another Chief. They now had two chiefs in two command vehicles but no fire engines. Understandably, when the fire started to run, you could hear the increasing urgency in their voices as they gave fire updates to County Dispatch and assigned the few arriving resources to point protection on structures. They were doing all they could do and doing it well. But, as we listed on our scanners, we knew they would not stop that fire.

The first two attack engines on the scene were Attack 39 (A39) and Attack 310 (A310), both arriving at least 10 minutes after the chiefs. During those 10 minutes, the fire doubled to 5 to 7 acres.

Sitting at home and later at Station 96, we listened to the radio traffic on Spokane County's and DNR's Dispatch channels. This is something we've done many times in the past. In most cases like this, the local district is optimistic about stopping the fire. However, seldom is DNR optimistic. This fire was a classic case in point.

AR 7404 was one of the first DNR engines dispatched at 2:41 PM. They had an ETE (estimated time of engagement) of 40 minutes. Within 10 minutes of being dispatched, AR 7404 could see the smoke column on the horizon and requested two Fire Bosses for air attack. Although it would take him another 22 minutes to arrive on the scene, it was clear to him that a ground attack by the district crews would not stop the fire. This kind of clarity is always more valuable than optimism because it comes from lots of experience fighting small fires that turn into large fires.

When the two Fire Bosses ordered by AR 7404 finally arrived on the scene, it was 3:36 PM, and the fire was estimated at over 30 acres. Everyone then realized the two Fire Bosses would not stop the fire. Instead, the planes were used to save homes. Their efforts would be limited to dropping their 500-gallon loads on fire surrounding threatened structures, not the running flanks or head of the fire front that was running and spotting to the northeast. At this point, Command realized they needed more to stop the fire. They needed a couple of "heavies" with thousands of pounds of retardant. They asked for one VLAT and two additional Fire Bosses at 3:15 PM. At 3:25 PM, they clarified with dispatch that they needed two heavies, not one, along with the two additional Fire Bosses. The fire was well over 100 acres when those air resources arrived overhead.

Don, Matt, and I had been texting each other and predicted that SCFD3 needed air support when the fire was three to five acres, and they had yet to get any engines on the scene. So we were impressed and relieved when AR 7404 took the initiative to order the Fire Bosses when he did. But we knew it would not be enough.

Over the years, one of the standing jokes at Station 96 when critiquing the initial attacks on fires in other districts, is mimicking the often-heard radio communication from first-in engines that goes something like this, "If we only had one more brush truck, we could stop this thing!" It's a joke because we've often heard this, or some version of it, from the initial attack crews on numerous fires in various districts whenever Red Flag conditions exist. Once you hear that phrase, you know the fire will probably go big. This is because not everyone on these crews has the experience and situational awareness to think beyond what they see. Red flag conditions accelerate the fire spread rate exponentially, and air support takes at the very least 30 minutes to get on the scene. Therefore, the picture you need is of where the fire will be in 30 to 60 minutes, not the picture of what's in front of you when you pull up and give your windshield size up.

While we listened to those initial attack crews arriving one at a time, only to be assigned structural point protection, we became certain Command would soon be requesting numerous strike teams of brush trucks and engines from neighboring districts to try and stop the fire's progression.

At 3:08 PM, we heard Command report that Cheney Brush 1 (CB1) was being abandoned by its crew. They were out of danger, but at 3:13 PM, Command reported the abandoned brush truck was on fire and fully involved. We decided to head to Station 96 and hang out just in case we got the call to go.

It was about 6:45 PM when Matt suggested Captain Don contact SCFD9's 920 Officer and let him know our crew was standing by at Station 96 and ready to go. The fire had just jumped Rock Lake Road, and it seemed the current resources were being stretched past their limit. We wanted to help.

Don agreed, and about five minutes after he had sent his text to 920, we were added to the fire. It was 6:59 PM. The fire was over 300 acres, and over 100 structures were reported threatened.

Matt, Don, and I were at the station when we got the call, but Jon was still at work. So we loaded Jon's gear in B96 and picked him up at a designated spot on our way to the freeway. Once we had Jon aboard, off we went. We were happy to be going but also a bit nervous about fighting such an active fire through the night in territory we had never seen while working under the command of officers we didn't know.

The Williams Lake Fire was burning 50 miles southwest of Station 96, and our travel time was about 50 minutes. As we sped east on I-90 and several county highways, we listened to nonstop radio traffic of units on the fire. The one-acre spot fire east of Rock Lake Road had quickly grown to over 40 acres, and by 7:43 PM, when we arrived, the fire also jumped Long Road, putting another group of structures in danger.

We had planned to report to the central staging area at Williams Lake Road; that's standard procedure. However, to get to Williams Lake Road, we had to drive south on Rock Lake Road and go past the intersection of Long Road, where the fire threatened unprotected residences. Once we realized this, Don radioed Incident Command and told him of our location. We were immediately assigned to Zulu Division and structure protection on Long Road. We arrived at the intersection of Rock Lake Road and Long Road at 7:59 PM and were told by Zulu Command, "Drive south on Long Road and find a structure to protect."

As we turned south on Long Road, we all laughed about the vague nature of the assignment. Our collective experience on a structure protection assignment has been you get a specific address and detailed instructions on what Command wants you to achieve. Not tonight. It looked like we were going to "John Wayne-it" all night.

As we headed south on Long Road, we passed several residences on the east side of the road that had fire approaching through the timber and brush from both the south and east. But each residence already had an engine protecting them. At one of the houses, we could see Brush 93 (B93), also from SCFD9, and we wondered aloud who was on the crew. All the residences appeared to have been evacuated, which was good news. It's understandable when homeowners try to make a stand and protect their homes, but it can end badly. We were glad to see the locals had left.

Most of the land between and behind these structures was thick with a 50-foot-tall Ponderosa Pine and a grass and brush understory. It was all well-cured fuel. If the fire had gone through this area earlier in the day, when the humidity was lower and the winds higher, we doubted if any of it would have survived. As we moved south, the smoke ominously got thicker and thicker.

Soon, we ran into Battalion Chief 2 from Spokane City Fire (BC2). The Chief had blocked the road with his pickup truck. He told us he was closing the road because the fire was now on both sides and was too dangerous. He said he wasn't sending anyone farther south on Long Road. So, we turned around and returned to the closest structure, intending to prep and defend it.

Pumper Tender 31 (PT31) from SCFD3 was already at the residence. We had a face-to-face with their crew and came up with a plan. They covered the south side of the residence, so we took the east and north sides. The west side faced Long Road and, at this point, was not threatened. It was 8:30 PM. The sight, sound, and heavy smell of the fires enveloped us.

We did our usual quick prep of the structure by moving outdoor furniture, toys, and other flammable stuff scattered through the large yard away from the house, garage, and outbuildings. We also located some 3/4 inch garden hose and hooked it up to a frost-free hydrant to use as an extra hoseline for small spot fires that might start near the house and deck.

The fire surrounding the property sat in the timber and brush about 40 yards away. It felt like we were in a classic gunfight in the movies with two antagonists staring at each other in the middle of the street. Perhaps the fire was sizing us up before it made a run toward the house.

It was also getting dark fast, and the smoke was coming from all around us, not just the fire we could see. Yet, there wasn't much else we could do except wait for the fire to come to us. We had a designated escape route and a safety zone about 1/2 mile north along Long Road. Although we were apprehensive, we were not concerned about what would come. A short time later, another District 3 resource, Pumper Tender (PT33), pulled into the driveway and set up on the north side of the property.

Jon and I decided to walk around to the front of the house to chat with Don and Matt. They had prepped the front yard and were waiting for the fire to approach. Just then, the BC2 drove to the house in his pickup and yelled at us. "Hey, you guys wanna save a house?"

We figured the house we were on was well protected with PT31 and PT33, so Don gave him the thumbs up and replied, "Sure." BC2 yelled back, "Follow me!"

We quickly reeled in our attack line, jumped in B96, and followed his pickup down the driveway and south on Long Road. About 1/4 mile south, his pickup disappeared into heavy smoke that was being blown across the road from the west. We quickly rolled up our windows and followed him into the smoke.

"Can you see where you're going, Matt?" Don asked.

"Yeah, I can just make out his taillights."

"This no longer feels like such a great idea," I said.

A collective chuckle let me know they were thinking the same thing. Don's response was his typical sarcastic, "Ya think?" That also made us laugh.

We continued driving slowly and watching those two small red taillights. About two minutes later, the visibility increased to about 50 yards. We could see numerous fires on both sides of the road, crawling through the thick brush and timber. The sky had grown quite dark, and the woods on both sides of the road were bursting with bright orange clusters of fire.

We followed BC2 into a short driveway on the east side of the road and parked behind him by a residence and garage that were surrounded by a slow-moving fire in brush and grass. The fire was slowly making its way towards the structures. We piled out, I started the pump, and Matt and Jon pulled the attack line to extinguish the fires closest to the garage. Don and I then tended the hoseline, keeping it free of the multitude of obstacles in the yard and away from any hot piles of ash.

Once we got farther into the backyard, we could see the entire area was littered with automobile engines, old tires, wood piles, and a large assortment of junk, most of it actively burning or smoldering. The fumes coming off the stuff worried us enough that we did all we could to stay upwind of whatever was burning. We spent about 30 minutes working around the structures until we had a good 60-foot area between the structures and any active fire. That was about all we could do.

Thinking back on it, I still cannot fathom why people dump junk all over their property and leave it there for years. Every time I see this behavior, it reminds me of the idiom: one man's trash is another man's treasure. Sometimes, people are indeed strange.

The Battalion Chief was happy with our work and told us, "OK, now I want you guys to cruise up and down Long Road. Put out anything that needs putting out. I'll check back occasionally. Just don't get too far off the road. Stay close to your truck."

By now, it was pitch dark. The smoke was blotting out any potential light from the moon and stars. The only light was from fires and emergency lights, a combination of flickering orange and flashing red, blue, and white lights. It was spooky and mesmerizing all at the same time.

There were three residences on the west side of Long Road and six on the east side. The Chief pointed out one driveway on the west side and told us not to go up it because it was too tight and overgrown with unburnt fuel. He had been up earlier in the daylight, and he was afraid we wouldn't be able to get in and out safely.

A second residence on the west side had a closed gate across the driveway. It had large signs stating it was "PRIVATE PROPERTY" and everyone should "KEEP OUT!" The Chief told us that earlier in the afternoon, the homeowner had come down to his gate carrying a shotgun and wearing a pistol. He told everyone who approached to stay off his property. The Sheriff had been called in, and he convinced the homeowner to go back to his house and stop walking around yelling at the firefighters while waving his shotgun around. If he didn't, he'd be going to jail. We figured the homeowner probably had an illegal pot farm or some other nonsense going on up by the house, so we agreed it was best to leave him be. He was now on his own as far as we were concerned. That left us with seven structures to patrol along about three-quarters of a mile of road.

It was about 9:30 PM when we started driving up and down Long Road, putting out spotfires along the roadside and around structures. The fire seemed to be building its momentum on the west side of the road and would occasionally run up to the road and spot across to the east side. In those instances, we'd park north of the fire so we could escape back to the intersection of Long Road and Rock Lake Road and then knock down all the spots that popped up on the east side of the road.

At about 11:00 PM, the fire on the west side of Long Road made a significant run towards the road. It had gotten into some dry ladder fuels and then moved into the crown of a tight group of 50-foot-tall Ponderosa Pine. In a roar and a flash, the trees began torching as the fire moved forward about 40 yards to the edge of the road and showered us with a mass of large embers. The embers were swarming and swirling all around, eventually landing on the east side of the road and starting numerous spotfires. The heat from the crown fire was alarming as it moved through the trees, only to stall when it hit the edge of a treeless powerline corridor. During this massive run of fire, there was a moment or two when we all thought it might be time to jump in the truck and retreat north to safety, but then the crown fire collapsed from a lack of new fuel. We then knew we could stay and chase down the spotfires.

Once we soaked all the spots, Jon and Matt put a wet line along the powerline corridor as far as they dared. This halted the advancing ground fire that accompanied the dying crown fire. The whole sequence lasted about 30 minutes, but it was an intense and extreme example of fire behavior none of us had ever seen before this late in the evening. It was a lesson well learned and remembered.

It eventually became necessary to fill up with water. We picked up our hoseline and drove north back to the Rock Lake and Long Roads intersection to fill up from one of the water tenders. After filling up, we headed south and resumed our patrol along Long Road. It was getting late, and we were getting tired, but we needed to get back to work. When we arrived, most of the trucks that had been protecting structures on Long Road had moved back to Rock Lake Road and were making sure the fire didn't jump it and head north. We seemed to be the only crew working Long Road.

While heading south, we spotted a small outbuilding that was fully involved about 50 yards off the east side of the road. We decided to drive into it and knock down the fire as it tried to spread to a nearby residence. The outbuilding turned out to be a total loss, but we were able to knock down enough fire from the surrounding brush until we were confident the fire wouldn't spread to the house. Just as we were finishing up, the gas motor on our pump stalled. Try as we might, we couldn't get it to run for more than 30 seconds before it stalled again. We had no choice but to head back to the staging area and explain our situation to Command.

It took a while, but eventually, Don was able to talk to Command, and the decision was made that we would have to call it a night and head back to Spokane. It was 1:36 AM, and our time on the Williams Lake Fire was over. We were okay with that. While we had been working on Long Road, a significant number of additional resources had moved into the area. We felt they had it covered. A few days later, the SCFD9 maintenance shop discovered that the fuel line from the gas tank to our pump was plumbed incorrectly and had to be altered. This was the first real test of B96 since we received it earlier in the summer, so we were glad it didn't happen during a more intense situation.

Fighting the Williams Lake Fire was a far different experience than most of our fires. Usually, we are one of the first crews on the scene and either have the fire knocked down by nightfall or get relieved by crews that come in for the night shift. This time, we joined the initial attack late in the day and saw a lot of extreme fire behavior when a fire usually "lays down for the night" because the temperature drops, the winds die, and the humidity rises. It was a great experience to work on extremely active fire behavior at night. We'll probably not forget the lessons it gave, which makes us all better prepared when something similar comes along and makes an evening run through the foothills of Mount Spokane. Now, that would be a career fire. However, to be honest, I'd be fine if it never happened.

Chapter 22

I Know I Fucked Up.
I Just Want to Go Home and Go to Bed.

Two days ago, I was sitting on the couch with Tyson, one of our Boxers, and talking to my wife, Karie, when my Apple Watch pinged with a notification of an MVA on Forker Road. The call came in as a 46B, meaning it was unknown if there were significant injuries. I got up, told Karie I had an MVA, kissed her goodbye, and headed for our RZR side-by-side to ride to the station.

It was Sunday, March 5th, at 5:20 PM, and we still had about six inches of soft melting snow on the ground, making the trip slow with lots of sliding around on the bumps and turns. When I got to the station four minutes later, I found Captain Don in his PPE, standing in the truck bay, loading his gear into the back seat of Engine 96. I dressed in my PPE as quickly as possible and climbed into the driver's seat.

We rolled out of the bay with lights and sirens. I needed to make a sharp left on Peck Road and an immediate right to enter Forker Road heading north.

"Am I good?" I asked, unable to see if any traffic was coming northbound on Peck.

"Clear-no wait!" Don replied.

I stopped abruptly at the end of the ramp. A woman in a small SUV crossed in front of us, heading north on Peck. I guess she didn't notice us in our 15-ton, 11-foot-tall red fire engine with lights and sirens rolling down the ramp.

"You're clear now," Don said.

I floored the accelerator and waited for the big turbo diesel to respond. Slowly, we started to accelerate as we headed north on Forker Road.

Don then called Dispatch.

"Dispatch. Engine 96 responding with two."

Dispatch replied, "Engine 96 with two. Engine 96, you have a one-vehicle rollover with possible minor injuries. Engine 94 and AMR 121 are also responding."

"Engine 96 copy."

Don turned to me. "Don't forget we're running cables."

"Yeah, I got it. I almost forgot, though. You can't feel it like you can the chains on the brush," I said as I eased off the accelerator to keep our speed under 35 mph. The snow on Forker had melted during the afternoon, so we were running cables on bare asphalt. Any faster than 35 mph, those cables start falling apart.

The accident scene was listed on our pager as the intersection of North Forker Road and East Foothills Road, about two miles north of the station. Don then got a text from Jereme, one of our newer volunteers, stating he was already on the scene POV, and there were no injuries. We saw the accident scene as we came around the last corner before Foothills Road. Dirt and debris were all over the road. Jereme's pickup was parked in the southbound lane just north of a late-model Jeep SUV that was on its wheels but looked like it had rolled a couple of times. I parked E96 on Forker, blocking the scene from the south.

"Dispatch, Engine 96," Don said into the mic.

"Dispatch." They replied.

"Engine 96 is on the scene. We have one car off the road on its wheels. We'll be checking for injuries and blocking the southbound lane of Forker. Engine 96 will be Forker Command."

I put the truck in neutral, pulled the parking brake, and climbed out. My first job was patient care, so I focused on checking the driver for injuries; I could see the car was heavily damaged, indicating what we call "a possible high mechanism for injury." This made it essential to get to the driver as soon as possible. I grabbed my turnout coat and helmet from the back seat of the engine, put them on, and headed to the other side of the truck to grab the BLS bag. Once I had the bag, I headed over to the crashed Jeep. Jereme walked past me, heading for E96.

"Driver's in the vehicle. He doesn't have any apparent injuries and doesn't want our help," he said with a sarcastic smile. I just nodded.

As I approached the car, I could see the roof was partially crushed, the windshield was smashed, the hood and grille were crushed, and bits of plastic and glass were spread across the road and around the car. The driver's side door was hanging open, and I could see the door-curtain airbags around the entire car had deployed during the accident. They were all hanging down to the middle of the door windows, which were intact and closed. I put my bag down and knelt on the ground so I could see under the deflated airbag on the driver's door and see the driver. I noticed the steering wheel airbag had not deployed and reminded myself not to get in front of it in case it deployed unexpectedly.

"Hi, I'm with the Fire Department. How are you doing?"

"I know I fucked up. I just want to go home and go to bed," the driver said slowly.

He sat still, looking forward through the smashed windshield, and was disgusted with himself. I noticed he wasn't wearing a seatbelt. But he was wearing a baseball cap with the bill pulled down over his eyes. He had no visible injuries, so I figured he was wearing a seatbelt when he crashed and must have taken it off.

"I understand. Were you wearing your seatbelt when you crashed?" I asked.

"Yeah. We don't need any help. We're OK."

"You said we. Was someone else in the car with you?"

"We don't need any help!"

I looked throughout the car and saw no evidence of another passenger. By now, I felt the driver was either very drunk, on drugs, or both. He was also not happy we were there. I think he was trying to deny the reality that he would get arrested. I felt a bit of empathy for him, but I also felt he deserved whatever was coming his way when the Sheriff showed up.

"Do you mind if I assess you? You know, measure your heart rate and take your blood pressure?"

"No. You're not gonna do that," he replied.

"OK. I understand. Do you have any pain?"

He shook his head no.

In the meantime, Engine 94 had pulled up, and their medic, Austin, had walked up to the car and stood just to my right.

"Who the fuck is that?" The driver said, startled by Austin's approach and ducking his head to try and look at Austin from under the airbag curtain.

"It's just another firefighter," I said.

"Fuck! I don't need you guys," he repeated.

I turned to Austin, "He's AOB,[5] but doesn't have any obvious injuries. He does *not* want to be assessed."

Austin smiled, shook my hand, said thanks, and we changed places. Well, this is his problem now, I thought. I picked up our BLS bag, turned to Tom, the officer from E94, and told him the same thing I had told Austin.

"Anyone else in the car," Tom asked.

"Nope, just him."

Tom nodded as I walked by him and over to E96 to put the BLS bag back in the truck.

Engine 94 was parked right behind E96, so the northbound lane was open while the southbound lane was blocked. Jereme was standing on the side of the road just south of the accident scene in an emergency vest he had gotten from E96. I grabbed a traffic sign and walked over to give it to him.

"So, I guess this is my new job?" He said, grinning.

"Yup, I'll do the other end," I said, grinning back.

I grabbed another traffic sign from E96, donned an emergency vest, and walked north to direct traffic at that end of the scene.

While I was talking with Jereme, Tom had walked over to Don and asked, "Can you ask Dispatch if the Sheriff's coming code? The driver's drunk and getting angry."

Don nodded and keyed his mic. "Dispatch, Forker Command."

"Go for Dispatch."

"Is the Sheriff coming code?"

"That's negative. A car is on the way from Trent and Flora, but they're not code."

"Could you upgrade them to code, please? This is a possible DUI, and the driver's getting belligerent."

"Copy up the code."

Jereme and I directed traffic past the accident scene for the next five minutes. When the Sheriff arrived, he walked over to the car and got an update from Austin. Austin was concerned that because of the intensity of the crash, he wanted the driver transported to the hospital, regardless of what the driver wanted. Austin explained that because of the driver's intoxicated condition

---

5 AOB is an abbreviation for "alcohol on breath," but it's often used more generally to indicate a person is under the influence of drugs or alcohol.

and the severity of the crash, the driver couldn't make an informed decision regarding his health. The Sheriff agreed. During the next five minutes, while the Sheriff talked to the driver, the AMR unit arrived, and their medic and EMT brought over a gurney.

The Sheriff addressed the driver. "I want you to get out of the car, walk over to that gurney, and sit on it."

"No, I'm not doing that," was the reply.

"Listen, you need to get out of the car, walk over to that gurney, and sit on it," he repeated more firmly.

The driver slowly climbed out of the car, took several steps, and stumbled. He turned and looked at his car. "Oh, shit," he said. "Can I look at my car?"

"No. Walk over to the gurney and sit on it."

The AMR crew moved the gurney closer to the car as the driver stumbled over and sat. "Do you have any weapons, sharp objects, or knives?" The AMR medic asked the driver. This is a standard question that is asked before a conscious patient is loaded onto the gurney, but in this case, the medic had seen two ammo clips hanging on the driver's belt, which certainly justified the question.

The driver reached for his belt and then turned to the Sheriff and said angrily, "Hey, where's my fucking gun?"

"You had a gun?" the Sheriff asked.

"Did you take my gun?" the driver replied loudly.

Soon, everyone was looking for the gun. They searched the car, the street, and along the ditches. It had gotten dark, and now everyone had their flashlights out, flashing them under the trucks and into the ditches and tall grass. I was still directing traffic when I saw the search begin. I wasn't sure what it was all about. Soon, Tom walked towards me, shining his flashlight along the ditch.

"What are you looking for, Tom?" I asked.

"A gun," he replied.

"Oh, nice," I said sarcastically. "It's probably still at the bar where he was drinking."

Tom just shook his head as he headed back to the AMR unit. Tom is a man of few words, and I could see he was more than ready to leave this mess to the Sheriff.

As Tom walked away, I wondered how someone could be as stupid as that driver. My second thought was: I've got to be more careful. This call could have gone very badly, in an unlimited number of ways, if that guy had his gun on his lap or in his hand.

I have no idea what eventually happened to that driver. My guess is they'll do a blood draw at the hospital, find it positive for one thing or another, and he'll end up in jail for the night. I hope he won't be driving through the Foothills anytime soon.

Thinking about this call the other night reminded me of a call I was on in the late 90s. I was first on the scene in my personal vehicle for a one-car rollover on Forker Road, just south of Station 96. The car ended up in a freshly plowed field on its side. A woman was lying about 50 feet from the car in the plowed dirt. She had not been wearing a seat belt and was thrown from the car. Various items, including a car seat for a baby, were scattered about the area. I scanned the field for the baby, then ran to the car and searched it. I found nothing. I returned to the woman. Her eyes were closed, so I knelt and asked loudly, "Did you have a baby in the car?"

"No, no, baby. I just wanna get sober," she said, never opening her eyes.

I looked her over for injuries and saw that her left foot was angled off at about 90 degrees from her leg. It was apparent she had a classic tib-fib bootstrap fracture. More simply, both bones in her leg were severely broken just above the ankle. Well, at least she *wants* to get sober, I thought.

Today, I can only hope the guy driving that Jeep on Forker Road feels the same way. I'm not optimistic he does.

Chapter 23

Line of Duty Death

It was a Friday morning in August of 2021 when we learned of the death of Lieutenant/Paramedic Cody Traber. You might remember from earlier chapters that Cody took over Command from Captain Don on the Macmahan fire, took Command of the Whipple Fire, and saved several homes from fire on the Wellsely Fire as the officer on B92. I distinctly remember standing in the empty truck bay at Station 96, where Brush 96 usually sits. I was waiting for Gary and Mark to return from a medical call because I had been slow getting to the station and missed the truck.

It was comfortably warm that morning, so I opened the bay door, grabbed a chair, and put it on the ramp to sit and wait for the guys to return. I first made a cup of coffee and then sat in the sun listening to one of our portable radios to help pass the time.

As is usual this time of year, the surrounding Foothills were stunning with their contrasting bright green pine forests, harvest-ready golden brown wheat fields, and brilliant blue and white sky. Sitting in the warm August sun, sipping my coffee, I was content.

At eleven minutes past eleven, my iPhone dinged. I reflexively pulled my phone from my pocket, tapping the message icon. It was a text from Captain Don to all the Station 96 volunteers. It contained an image and seven ominous words: "Just received this terrible news from Greg…" Oh, shit! I thought.

I could see the image in Don's text was a screenshot of a text Assistant Chief Greg Anderson had sent to Don. I pulled out my reading glasses and read it. It began: "There is no easy way to say this." In that instant, I knew I would read some terrible news, but I couldn't imagine what. My stomach tightened.

The text was 123 words, telling us that Cody fell to his death from a highway overpass the night before. He was the officer on E92 last night, and the crew was searching in the dark for a reported brush fire. They had stopped on an overpass to gain a better vantage point to spot the fire, and somehow, while Cody was walking along the bridge, he fell over the rail, plummeting over 100 feet through the darkness to the ground below. Greg and the crews on E92 and E91 found Cody's body below the overpass. It was clear Cody had died instantly from his injuries.

I was stunned. I couldn't believe it. It was too inexplicable to be true. But I knew it must be true. "What the fuck?" was all I could say, but there was no one with me to say it to.

I texted a reply to the group: "Fucking awful."

Just then, Mark and Gary returned, backed B96 onto the ramp, and climbed out.

"Have you guys read Don's recent text?" I asked.

"No, why?" Gary replied.

"You need to read it," was all I could say. I didn't want to try and explain.

Both Mark and Gary got out their phones and read the text from Don and then the text from Greg. They were equally stunned. We didn't know what to do or say. We all just stood on the ramp, asking each other how such a thing could happen.

Eventually, we talked about the odd early morning brush fire call Mark and Matt had gone to at 5 AM. The call came in as a 14H, as most brush fires do in the middle of August. But the location was about 10 miles west of the station, and the only Station 96 resource on the call was P96, our Jeep plow. When Matt and Mark left the station in P96, they were immediately asked by the 920 Officer on the scene to bring the water tender instead of P96. When they arrived on the scene with WT96, they found a Spokane City engine was already there, along with a 920 Officer that neither Mark nor Matt recognized. This was all unusual because units from Stations 91 and 92 should also have been there but were not. We later discovered they hadn't been dispatched to anything all morning. Mark mentioned that the SFD crew and 920 Officer seemed very subdued, which is not the usual demeanor of guys on a fire call. In addition, the 920 Officer appeared as if he had been up all night. It was an odd set of circumstances all around. The fire had already been knocked down, but it was still smoldering, so the 920 Officer told Matt and Mark to mind the fire until DNR showed up and then turn it over to them. The SFD engine and 920 quickly packed up and left. This was even more strange and unusual, to say the least. Matt and Mark did as they were told and eventually returned to Station 96 an hour later, a bit confused about the situation.

As we stood in the bay, knowing about last night's tragedy, things made sense. The 5 AM brush fire was, in fact, in the primary response areas of both Stations 91 and 92. But, because both crews had been on the call last night when Cody fell, those two stations had been taken out of service. The SFD engine and a replacement 920 Officer for Greg were now covering the area. Their odd behavior at the fire indicated they already knew about the tragedy.

As we remained in the bay and talked through the events of last night and this morning, several texts came in from our station volunteers. Everyone was shocked and saddened by the news. Over the years, we had all worked with Cody on fires and EMS calls. We also attended numerous training classes he taught at the SCFD9 training facility. He was well-liked and highly respected by all of us. His death affected us deeply and still does. He was only 41 years old.

Four days later, on August 31st, several of us from Station 96 participated in the procession that delivered Cody's body from the Spokane County Medical Examiner's office to a local funeral home in West Spokane. Don, Gary, Matt, Jon, and I took E96 and joined numerous local fire and law enforcement vehicles to transport him the four miles through downtown Spokane. The long procession began its journey by staging at the Medical Examiner's office in east Spokane. Firefighters from District 9 stood at attention and lined the walkway, forming an Honor Corridor from the ME's building to a waiting District 4 Fire Department ambulance. An honor guard, including six pallbearers of Cody's closest friends and colleagues, carried his flag-draped casket out to the waiting ambulance.

Standing at attention, we all watched the solemn, choreographed ritual of carrying the casket. The only sounds being made were the syncopated steps of the pallbearers and the muted calls of the commander of the honor guard guiding the march.

As I watched the ceremony, I could only think of the sorrow Cody's wife and four children must have felt as they stood silently just fifteen feet across from me. I almost lost it and broke down in tears at seeing them. How could they possibly deal with such tragedy? How could they ever find relief from the grief? I had to avert my gaze to an inanimate object across the way as I told myself to breathe, in and out, one breath at a time, to keep it together.

Once the ceremony ended, we all headed for our trucks to begin the journey. I was driving E96 as the procession wound its way through the streets. At various intersections, firefighters from Spokane Valley, District 8, and Spokane City Fire stood by their trucks at attention, saluting Cody and the entire procession. It was a very moving experience. We were glad to be a part of it, but during most of the ride, the cab of E96 was quiet. We all were still processing what we had lost and what we were a part of.

When we finally arrived at the funeral home, the scripted ritual was repeated as the casket was carried from the ambulance to the viewing room. Those who chose to could then say a personal goodbye. After the casket entered the memorial building, all the firefighters stood around awkwardly in their Class A uniforms, talking quietly in small groups. Several District 9 chiefs made their way through the groups, thanking everyone for coming and being part of the ceremony. It felt good to be able to talk with friends about Cody or talk about other things as a way of relieving the stress and pent-up emotions. Eventually, we were all allowed to enter the viewing room one at a time, each of us saying our private goodbye to Cody. There were very few dry eyes as firefighters left that room.

Those of us from Station 96 eventually gathered outside and walked slowly to E96. We took a group picture while standing by the engine, climbed in, and headed back to Station 96. On the return drive, we all admitted it had been emotionally draining, but we were glad to have been there, to have played our part in honoring Cody.

A bit earlier, while at the ceremony, District 9 Division Chief Bobby Shindelar spoke briefly to the group about Cody. These are some of his comments.

> Cody was the firefighter of firefighters. He was a great example of public service. He strived to do well in everything that he did, and he would go the extra mile by doing more than what was asked of him…. He had a passion for the work that he did and his commitment to teaching. He was just a tremendous person…. He was just one of those exceptional people. He had a good sense of humor, and everybody enjoyed being around Cody, and he enjoyed being with people.

Those of us who knew and worked with Cody felt the same. We'll miss him.

Several weeks after Cody's memorial, we each received a set of red vinyl stickers of the Maltese Cross with Cody's name on it. In the center of the cross is the number 500, Cody's badge number. I put one of my stickers on the glass of the rear entry door to Station 96. The other, I put on the door that separates our turnout room from the engine bay. Now, every time we enter the building or head out to the engine bay to answer the call of duty, we are reminded of Cody, a firefighter's firefighter.

Chapter 24

Tourniquet

On a recent Saturday morning in November, 2023, I was sitting at the kitchen table reading about the day's Wind Warning for 25 to 30 mph gusts on my iPad when a trauma call popped up on the screen. The location of the call was the east end of Donner Rd, about two miles from the station. I turned to Karie, who was sitting in the living room knitting, and told her I had a trauma call. As I headed for the mudroom to grab my coat and helmet, I hoped I'd be back soon enough to go out to lunch with her as we had planned.

My ride to the station in our Polaris side-by-side was uneventful. I was quick enough that Captain Don and I arrived simultaneously. Walking through the dressing room, Don grabbed his heavy turnout coat, which surprised me.

"Why the turnouts?" I asked.

"The patient might be outside, and it's cold and windy. All they gave us was a general location on Donner, not a specific address," he replied.

Because I was already wearing two layers, an SCFD9 work shirt, and my jacket, I left my turnout coat on the hook and headed for B96. We were soon heading south on Forker Rd with lights and sirens. Don radioed Dispatch and told them we were responding in B96.

The call was on our North Primary radio channel. When Don signed on, two distinct conversations were happening with Dispatch. One conversation was with E94. The other was with E44 in District 4. Dispatch was telling E94 that Life Flight had been launched. We recognized Darin's voice as the officer on E94. Darin told Dispatch he could see several good spots to land the helicopter on his AVL's satellite view of the scene. Our 920 (duty officer) and 930 (safety officer) officers also radioed and asked Dispatch to add them to the call. The radio traffic then switched to the D4 call. We drove on, waiting for the District 4 radio traffic to pause and for Dispatch to reply with the customary short description of the call. The original page we received on our phones did not include a call for Life Flight. Something had changed.

The address was about a three-minute drive from the station, and when we were about halfway there, Don got tired of waiting for the short and radioed Dispatch.

"Dispatch, this is Brush 96. Could we have the short for this call?"

After a short delay, Dispatch replied. We were less than a half mile from the scene.

"Bruch 96, you have a 54-year-old male who completely severed his right arm in a sawmill accident. The helo is two to three minutes out. Also responding are 920 and 930."

"Brush 96 copy," Don replied.

"Tourniquet," I said to Don as an image of the tourniquet stashed in our BLS bag appeared in my mind. I also started rummaging in my coat pocket for my safety glasses, trying not to think about how much bleeding there would be.

"Copy that," Don replied.

As we approached the scene, we could see a woman at the end of the road frantically waving to us. She was holding a cell phone up to her ear with her other hand. We later learned she had been talking with Dispatch on the phone. She turned around and started running up the driveway back towards the house. As we approached her in B96, Don rolled down his window and asked, "Where's the patient?"

"He's at the sawmill," she replied, pointing to it. We could hear Life Flight's helicopter circling above. We've never had the bird beat us to a call. This was odd.

I drove quickly along the driveway, which took us to the right, passing below the large stand-alone sawmill. The four-foot diameter circular blade was stationary, and I could easily see the huge cutting teeth lining its perimeter. Once again, I fought the impulse to imagine what had happened. I also saw a man wearing a large cowboy hat kneeling on the other side of the mill. When I parked, I looked back at the mill and saw the patient lying prone and partially covered by a red blanket.

"I didn't see the patient, did you?" Don said.

"I see him. He's right behind the saw, lying on the ground." I replied.

I climbed out, trotted around the back of the truck, opened the EMS compartment, grabbed the BLS bag, and headed for the patient. Don headed towards the clearing below us to land the bird. Based on our call records, it had taken me nine minutes to get from my kitchen table to the patient's side.

The patient was lying in a large pile of sawdust, covered with a throw blanket. The man wearing a cowboy hat was kneeling by the patient's head and holding his left hand. There were two bloody white towels on the ground next to the patient. I dropped the BLS bag, grabbed the tourniquet, and knelt by the patient's right side. A large farming tractor was parked ten feet to my right. A six to eight-foot-long power take-off (PTO) shaft with two universal joints extended from the tractor's rear power output to the transmission of the sawmill. I instantly recognized the setup. Sawmills are often powered by using a tractor's PTO. They are notoriously dangerous, and accidents involving them kill and maim dozens of people each year. I also saw clothing wrapped around one of the PTO's universal joints. I was surprised when I glanced at the saw blade and saw no blood. Neither the tractor nor the mill was running.

The patient was shirtless and partially covered by the blanket. I could see his left arm was severely bruised but intact. I couldn't see his right arm. At first, I thought he was lying on top of it. But as I knelt, I realized his right arm was missing. A white towel, covered in bits of sawdust and spotted with blood, covered the area where his shoulder and upper arm *should* have been. I was amazed the wound wasn't bleeding profusely.

"What's the patient's name," I asked.

"Robert. I'm his brother." said the man in the hat.

"Is he conscious?"

"Yes."

"Robert, can you hear me," I said, bending over to speak to him. I could only see the left side of his face. His eye was closed, he was motionless, and he looked unconscious.

But he instantly replied, "Yes, I'm in a lot of pain."

"Robert, I'm with the Fire Department. We are going to help you. The helicopter is here, and they will take you to the hospital. Hang in there! We're going to do everything we can to help," I said.

Robert's brother had wrapped a towel around Robert's right shoulder area. A second towel covered the wound. Blood and sawdust contaminated both. I removed the towel that covered the wound, expecting to find a severed humerus, bleeding blood vessels and torn muscles. To my surprise, nothing was left of his arm or the joint. There was minimal bleeding. I turned to Robert's brother.

"Where's the arm?"

"Over there, wrapped up on the PTO," he replied.

"Get the arm! I want the arm," Robert said loudly.

"We'll get it, Robert, don't worry," I said.

All the pieces instantly fell into place. Robert's clothing had to have gotten caught in the universal joint of the PTO. The spinning PTO must have torn his arm off.

"He spun around the PTO at least twice before his arm came off," Robert's brother said calmly.

I rewrapped the shoulder area and applied direct pressure to the wound.

Don approached us, and I gave him a quick patient update.

"Fifty-four-year-old male, conscious and alert. Complete amputation of the right arm."

"Fifty-four-year-old male, conscious and alert," Don repeated. He then keyed his radio's mic and updated all incoming units.

Gary, who had arrived POV, suddenly appeared on my left.

"What do you need," he asked.

"See if you can get a blood pressure. No, wait. Just try and get a pulse and oxygen sat," I said.

Robert's left forearm and hand were very pale from the massive vasoconstriction that was counteracting his bleeding and shock. We were not surprised when Gary couldn't get a reading on the pulse oximeter.

Robert suddenly spoke. "I was an EMT for 20 years. I'm telling you, I'm going into shock. I'm in a lot of pain."

I knew Robert was right. He was going into shock.

"Hang in there, Robert. We're doing everything we can," I said.

I looked up to see the two-man crew from Life Flight coming around the sawmill. I quickly gave them the patient's condition and told them what had happened.

The flight nurse asked me, "Did you get a tourniquet on it yet?"

"No. There's nothing to put it on," I replied.

"Let's try again," he said.

I removed the towels as we rotated Robert to expose his shoulder area. I expanded the tourniquet and placed it around the wounded area.

"Nope, that's not going to work. Just continue with direct pressure," the nurse said.

He stood up and moved to the head of the patient, asking Robert's brother to step away.

The paramedic from the helicopter knelt beside me to my left. He tried reaching across the patient to start an IV on Robert's left hand but soon realized the veins were too constricted to canulate.

"Let's just get the stretcher and load him," the nurse said.

Gary and the medic quickly retrieved the stretcher and positioned it so we could roll the patient over on his left side, keeping the wound out of the sawdust. While we waited for the stretcher, Darin, the officer on E94, asked us questions about Robert's medical history, allergies, and current medications. When Gary reappeared with the stretcher, the nurse led the count as we log-rolled Robert onto it. I gently guided Robert's left arm out from under him.

"Hold it right there so I can start an IV," the medic said.

I did as he asked, holding Robert's left arm with my left hand while maintaining pressure on his right shoulder with my right. The reality of how quickly our lives can be changed forever struck me with inescapable clarity.

The medic quickly established a patent venous catheter.

While we were working on Robert, the crews from E94 and AMR searched for the missing arm. They found it 20 feet from the PTO on the other side of the sawmill. It was intact. They double-bagged it and surrounded it with all the cold packs they had.

We moved Robert and his severed arm to the helicopter. Soon, the bird and its occupants were in the air and on their way to the hospital. Their travel time was less than five minutes. They had been on the ground for less than 18 minutes.

As I walked away from the LZ, I suddenly felt cold and started to shiver. I had been kneeling in damp sawdust that had been sucking the heat out of my legs. My pants were wet and spotted with blood from my knees down to my shoes. My gloves, shoes, and jacket sleeves were also damp and contaminated with blood. It was time to decontaminate my clothes, dry off, and head back to the station.

Before we left the scene, the crew on E94, Rob (our Safety Officer), Don, Gary, and I met for a brief tail-board discussion. Darin explained that Life Flight arrived so quickly because they were in the air returning to their base when they received the call from Dispatch. Because of the nature and location of the call, they diverted to our scene. We were incredibly fortunate they did because had they not been in the air, they would have refused to launch from their base due to the weather conditions (15-plus mph winds and gusts to 25 mph). Darin pointed out that if Life Flight had not been available, things could have gone very differently. The bottom line was we got lucky and were prepared to use that luck to benefit the patient.

During the remainder of the debrief, Rob focused on how we felt. Don, Gary, and I knew from experience that it's not easy to see a tragic event like this without being affected. But we also knew that talking about it with trusted, experienced colleagues like Rob and the crew on E94 always helps. After the debrief, Gary left for home, and Don and I headed for B96. As I approached the driver's side door, I saw the patient's brother and the woman who waved us in, sitting quietly on a bench not far away.

I asked them, "How are you folks doing?"

"We're okay," the woman said, sounding unsure.

"Everyone did everything they could. We're all hoping for the best," I said.

"Thank God for all you firefighters," she replied.

Then she looked up and yelled loudly to E94's crew, who were climbing into their truck across the driveway. "Thank God for all you firefighters!"

Chapter 25

Are Volunteer Firefighters an Endangered Species?

When I joined Station 96 in 1996, we had 20 volunteers. Since then, our numbers have slowly decreased as older volunteers retired and younger volunteers either got hired as career firefighters or moved away.

In 1996, SCFD9 had roughly 120 volunteers and 30 career personnel. In 2023, we have about 73 career personnel (including nine chiefs) and 20 active volunteers. That's an 83.3% *decrease* in volunteers and a 41% *increase* in career firefighters. If this pattern continues, volunteers will be extinct in SCFD9 very soon.

Station 96 is now down to six active volunteers in 2023. Three of our volunteers, including myself, are in their late 60s. Lieutenant Gary is 67, Captain Don is 67, and I am 68. The three of us will likely be retired by the time we are 70. I doubt we will find new volunteers to replace us. Although volunteers no longer staff every District station, as they did back in 1996, similar issues face the four all-volunteer stations: Stations 95, 96, 97, and 98. The remaining five stations, 91, 92, 93, 94, and 99, are staffed by career firefighters 24 hours a day, seven days a week. Station 94 is a hybrid of career and volunteers, with five volunteers. However, their only responsibility is to staff WT94 when fires occur in areas without fire hydrants. In their response area, this type of call probably happens less than five times a year. Of the four all-volunteer stations, Stations 95 and 98 are in high-density urban areas that are covered very effectively by career-staffed stations. Each of these stations has at most three or four active volunteers. Both stations are no longer called for EMS emergencies and quickly get canceled on MVAs by career-staffed engines that cover their area. Only Stations 96 and 97 have active volunteers who respond regularly to fire, EMS, MVAs, rescues, hazardous situations, and service calls. And although Station 97 has maybe six volunteers, only one is regularly active. More often than not, when they get a call, he responds by himself. So, why is this happening? In summary, only Station 96, which is down to six active volunteers, responds to the entire range of emergency calls and is regularly the first SCFD9 resource to arrive on the scene.

The main reason for the extinction of volunteers in SCDF9 is that the job has changed. For example, during the past ten years, 73% of emergency calls for Station 96 were EMS-related (i.e., medical/trauma/rescue). Fire calls were 21% of all calls. Consequently, we spend most of our time being EMTs. This is a big change from when volunteers in SCFD9 responded *only* to fires. Over the years, all SCFD9 stations have gotten busier. However, the data show that most calls require expertise in emergency medical services. Developing and maintaining the skills and expertise to do this work requires extensive initial and ongoing training, making it unappealing to most potential volunteers.

It is possible (but not highly probable) that recruits could be found to replace retiring volunteers at Stations 96 and 97. However, that would contradict local and national trends for small rural stations, departments, and districts. What follows is a local example, followed by a description of the national trends.

Spokane County Fire District 4 borders the northern border of District 9. SCFD4 covers 330 square miles of a primarily rural population of 45,000 residents. District 4 has ten fire stations, only five of which have a minimal number of full-time career staff. Some of their volunteers are paid to be on-call part-time; the remainder are non-paid volunteers. In 2016, SCFD4 built a new Station 48 to replace the old station, which was nothing more than an ancient two-bay wooden garage on Mount Spokane Park Highway. Station 48 has always been an all-volunteer station serving the upper foothills of Mt Spokane. It is situated about five miles north of Station 96. Unfortunately, a couple of years after the new station was built, it was de-certified as a District 4 Fire Station and had to be closed. This decertification happened because you must have a minimum of six volunteers to be certified. They were down to just a single volunteer, who was over 60 years old. And, because the station had a very low call volume, District 4 could not justify staffing it with paid firefighters.

The loss of Station 48 has been costly. For example, since Station 48 was de-certificated, Station 96 has increasingly responded as mutual aid to Station 48's first-in area. This is a good solution because we often have shorter response times than other District 4 stations, which are farther away. The increased opportunity to serve has also been welcomed by the volunteers at Station 96.

However, our responses serve an area that generates zero income for District 9. In addition, the decertification of Station 48 has raised premiums for local insurance rates. Is this the future for District 9 areas protected by Station 96 and 97? I hope not. But it's inevitable unless something is done about it.

Let's now look at what has been happening nationally. I created Figures 1 and 2 using data from the *US Fire Department Profile 2020* by R. Fahy, B. Evarts, and G. P. Stein, published by the National Fire Protection Association (NFPA) and published online in September 2022. The authors reported there were 1,041,200 firefighters in the US in 2020. Approximately 65% were volunteers (i.e., 676,900 volunteers).

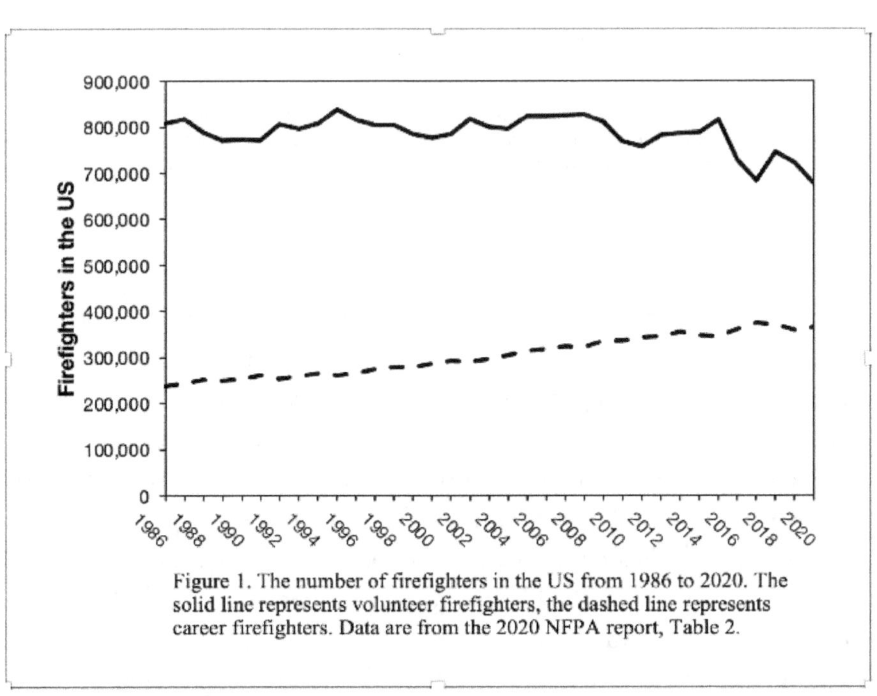

Figure 1. The number of firefighters in the US from 1986 to 2020. The solid line represents volunteer firefighters, the dashed line represents career firefighters. Data are from the 2020 NFPA report, Table 2.

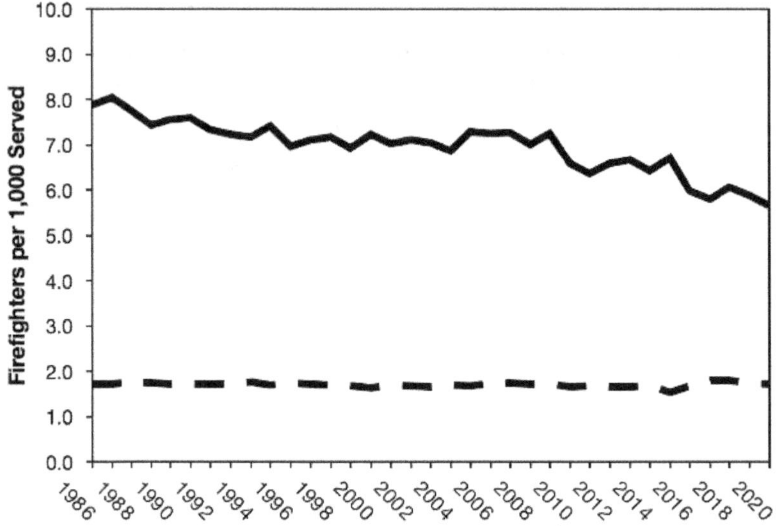

Figure 2. The number of US firefighters per 1,000 residents served from 1986 to 2020. The solid line represents volunteer firefighters, the dashed line represents career firefighters. Data are from the 2020 NFPA report, Table 2.

Figure 1 shows the number of US firefighters since 1986 when NFPA began collecting these data. As displayed in Figure 1, the data show that the number of volunteer firefighters began to decrease around 2008. In contrast, the number of career firefighters has grown steadily since 1986.

The data presented in Figure 2 show the number of firefighters per 1,000 individuals residing in the communities they protect. When presented in this manner, the data indicate that the number of volunteer firefighters per 1,000 people has *decreased* steadily. However, the number of career firefighters per 1,000 people has remained *constant*.

Figure 1 shows the absolute number of volunteers decreased by 16.2% between 1980 and 2020. But Figure 2 shows that the number of volunteer firefighters per 1,000 people served decreased a whopping 28% during that same period. Thus, the volunteer numbers *decreased* while the rural population they served *increased*. In contrast, the data show proportional gains in the number of career firefighters and the population they serve.

The first thing that needs to be done is to discover why volunteer numbers are decreasing. Two probable factors causing the ongoing losses of volunteers are 1) the increased retirement of aging volunteers and 2) the changing demographics of small rural communities.

Age-based cohort data contained in the 2020 FFPA report mentioned above (but not presented here) show that older, more experienced US firefighters are rapidly approaching retirement. When we dig a bit deeper into the NFPA report, it becomes apparent the most severe decreases are in volunteers, not career firefighters, and the decreases are happening primarily in the smallest communities. For example, the 2020 NFPA report presents the 2020 age profile of firefighters by the size of the community they served. The data show that in communities of less than 2,500 residents, 34% of the firefighters are over 50 years of age. Only 22% of the firefighters in these communities are under 30 years of age. That's a 12% disparity that might not seem important. But let's put it in context. The NFPA data also show that in larger communities, the percentage of volunteer firefighters under 30 exceeds those over 50 by about 6%. Therefore, there is an 18% disparity between what's happening in small communities (12% *fewer* young firefighters) versus large communities (8% *more* younger firefighters).

These patterns are troublesome because the smallest communities have the smallest call volumes and tax bases. Consequently, small communities can neither afford nor justify hiring and outfitting career fire stations to replace their disappearing volunteers. This is a very, very big problem.

According to the 2020 NFPA report, there were 29,452 fire departments in the US in 2020, and 47% (13,958) of them were all-volunteer departments serving communities of 2,500 or less. If we assumed those 13,958 departments, each served the maximum categorical 2,500 people, that's almost 35 million people (roughly 10% of the population of the US). Even if the actual median community size in this 2,500 or less category is 1,250 residents, that's 17.5 million people who are in danger of losing what little protection they had in 2020 because the number of volunteers is decreasing. Those statistics are alarming. But no alarm bells seem to be going off.

One past approach to obtaining and retaining fire protection in small communities is annexing into a larger neighboring fire district, or department, that already has career-staffed fire stations. That is what was done to create and maintain Station 96 in the Foothills. Yet, career stations of larger communities might have longer response times when traveling to small rural communities. However, as was done in SCFD9 in the 70s, the solution is not to *replace* local volunteer stations with distant career stations but to have *both* career and volunteer fire stations co-exist within the district. In this model, career stations are located in more densely populated areas with higher call volumes and tax bases, while volunteer stations are in less populated rural areas. When a call goes out in the rural area, both stations send a response. If the volunteers are not available, a career resource will always arrive at the scene, even if the response time is longer than we would like. If the volunteer station responds, the response time is shorter.

This approach has proved effective as long as the volunteer station has a sufficient number of volunteers and the career department or district has adequate funds to support the volunteer station. But what can be done when the volunteer station is losing its volunteers through retirement and attrition, as is happening at Station 96? Let's examine the history of Station 96 and District 9 in more detail to gain insights into the decreases in volunteer numbers.

As I presented in an earlier chapter, Station 96 was created by annexing the Foothills area by SCFD9 in the 1970s. The annexation resulted in the building of a small new fire station. The new station was a post and beam metal building with three bays, a bathroom, a well, and an above-ground 130,000-gallon cistern as a water supply. The bays were filled with surplus fire equipment and trucks until the early 1980s when SCFD9 purchased a new structural engine and water tender. The station also received a hand-me-down brush truck and a used Jeep plow.

A pivotal event for SCFD9 that benefited Station 96 and our Foothills community was the 1987 hiring of Chief Bob Anderson as the new Fire Chief for SCFD9. At that time, the district had seven fire stations spread across the district and had hired 12 additional career firefighters to add to its 100-plus volunteers. Because the District's equipment was outdated, and the stations were in poor condition, Chief Anderson created a new plan in 1992 for the district, which coincided with the voters of District 9 passing a $3.5 million bond. With the funds from this bond and subsequent levies, the Fire District built new versions of Stations 91, 92, and 93 in more optimal locations. Stations 95 and 96 were remodeled and expanded, and a new Station 94 was built on East Bigelow Gulch Road. Alongside the new Station

92, a new training center and administration building were also built. At that time, Stations 95, 96, 97, and 98 were all-volunteer stations. Stations 91, 92, 93, and 94 had a mix of volunteers and career firefighters. With vision and planning, SCFD9 transformed itself from a volunteer-based fire district to a hybrid career/volunteer model that could fund itself and meet the needs of both its urban and rural neighborhoods. It's a great story, but that was then, and this is now. This innovative and effective hybrid model needs an overhaul because it's losing its volunteers from the one place it needs them: the outer rural communities.

So, what's the solution? No one seems to know. It's important to consider that the original Foothill volunteers were grandfathered into the Fire District's cadre of firefighters. In those early years, the station only responded to fires, and the number of fires was few. However, after a few years, Fire District 9 began requiring all new volunteers complete formal firefighter and EMS training by attending a newly established Firefighter Academy and obtaining state and nationally recognized EMT certification (paid for by the Fire District). These requirements became necessary because of the expanding mission of the Fire District. For example, in the 70s and 80s, Station 96 responded only to fires. But, by 2011, Station 96 responded to 70 calls; 33 were EMS and 14 were MVA calls. Those 47 EMS/MVA calls were 67% of all calls. In 2021, we responded to 161 calls. We had 93 EMS and 17 MVAs, equaling 68% of all calls. Thus, over two-thirds of the work we've been doing during the past decade wasn't even a part of the Station's mission back when it was commissioned. Because of these call-related changes, volunteer firefighters' expectations, professionalism, and time commitments have increased dramatically, which is not a local phenomenon. Let's take a brief look at the national data.

In the US, during 1980, fires were 28%, and medical aid/rescue calls were 46% of all calls. In 2020, only 5% of all calls were fires, while 65% were medical/rescue. Mutual aid calls increased slightly from 2.5% in 1980 to 3.8% in 2020.[6] It is clear that the mission of fire departments throughout the US has expanded as we provide an increasing amount of out-of-hospital medical care. Indeed, 96% of departments serving more than 100,000 residents provide both BLS and ALS services. Why? Because it is needed.

---

6 Additional categories of calls include false alarms, hazardous materials/conditions, and others.

However, for communities of 2,500 or less, only 6% provide ALS, and 49% provide BLS service. I am sure those smaller departments that do not provide any EMS support would like to, but it would cost them time and money they do not have, and even fewer local individuals would likely volunteer.

So, in the end, are volunteer firefighters becoming extinct? The answer for District 9 is yes, and I am convinced it's also the case in small communities throughout the US. As I stated earlier, part of the problem is the changing demographics of small rural communities. In such communities, younger people tend to move elsewhere to start families and careers. At the same time, middle-aged community members who have moved into the rural community to build dream homes and escape the city probably don't understand the need and benefits of volunteering. Or perhaps they can't find the time for the expanded firefighter and EMS training and certifications. The bottom line is that the problem is real, affects millions of people, and will get worse before it gets better. Fire departments, districts, and communities, both large and small, need to fully recognize the problem and develop a vision and commitment to find a solution quickly. One solution won't fit all situations, but we must find a way to ensure our communities are protected. I fear that few are aware and actively trying to solve these issues at a time when the need for fire and EMS first responders continues to rise. If you live in a small rural community, the ball is in your court.

Epilogue

It's the fall of 2023, and I am preparing the final touches on this book. When I started writing these stories, I was sure I would be retiring from Fire District 9 at the end of 2023. But as that time approaches, I am hesitating. In February this past winter, I committed to improving my fitness so I could work the fire season without any physical issues. I did this by changing my diet and starting a daily routine of yoga and strength exercises. I also continued to get my 10,000 steps each day and tried to get eight hours of sleep each night. Consequently, I have lost 18 pounds and gotten stronger and much more flexible. I feel ten years younger. So, I am asking myself: why not carry on?

There are also other important reasons I am hesitating to retire. A major one is that there are six of us left at Station 96. For us to get a truck out the door and head to a call, we need two firefighters on the truck. When a call comes in, we usually only get two volunteers who can respond, and one of those is me. If I stop, I imagine the number of instances the truck never leaves the bay, or many minutes later, will increase significantly. I'd hate to see that happen. Another important reason I am hesitating is that I like doing the work, and I like doing it with my brothers. What should I do? I am not sure.

I am also beginning to hesitate because I am thinking about what happened this summer and what might happen in the future.

This past August, we had two devastating fires within 30 miles of the Foothills. We were not sent to fight those fires, but we listened intently to our radios and scanners as each fire consumed over 10,000 acres. The Oregon Fire, 30 miles northwest of the Foothills, burned 10,817 acres and destroyed 126 primary homes and 258 outbuildings. The Gray fire, which was 30 miles to the southwest, burned 10,085 acres and destroyed most of the city of Medical Lake. Over 185 residences were lost. Miraculously, there was only one fatality on each fire. Both fires started on the same day, August 18, and were human-caused. The two fires were stoked by Red Flag conditions: high winds, high temperatures, and low humidity. Those of us living in the Foothills could see the vast columns of smoke from the fire, and we smelled the smoke for days. On the morning of the second day of the Oregon Fire, I found a smattering of ash spread across our property and the surrounding woodlands. Overnight, a shift from the southwest to the north had also brought the smoke from the hundreds of fires burning in western Canada south to Spokane County.

Consequently, Spokane's air quality was in the hazardous range for two days. All these events left a lasting impression on many of us living in the Foothills. I believe we are living on borrowed time. Something like this or worse than these local large fires can easily happen in the Foothills. If it does, I want to be here to help. So, for now, at least, I will go day-by-day, call-by-call, and continue to do the work until my body tells me it's time to stop.

Acknowledgments

There are many people I must thank who made it possible for me to write this book. First and foremost is Karie, my wife. Her love and support during my many years of volunteering have been unwavering. In addition, her enthusiasm for my writing the book has motivated me all the more, especially when it was only a pipe dream. I love you, and thank you for supporting me all these years.

Next, I thank all the current and past volunteers at Station 96 that have made my experience so positive. Most importantly, I thank those mentioned in the book, some of whom still answer the call day and night. Without your willingness to meet with me repeatedly and rehash our calls, remembering what I had forgotten or gotten wrong, the book would not exist. These brothers of mine also showed a surprising willingness to read my early drafts (No matter how bad they were!) and give invaluable input. Go Fighting 96!

Lastly, I thank all those volunteers and career firefighters in District 9 who have supported the crew's efforts at Station 96 over the years. Your support matters to us at Station 96 much more than you know.

And finally, I thank my dad. I doubt I would have ever become a firefighter if he had not served for 20 years in Providence, R.I. I wish he had lived long enough to share our stories over a hot cup of coffee or a cold beer.